Harvard
Business
Review

ON

CORPORATE

GOVERNANCE

THE HARVARD BUSINESS REVIEW PAPERBACK SERIES

The series is designed to bring today's managers and professionals the fundamental information they need to stay competitive in a fast-moving world. From the preeminent thinkers whose work has defined an entire field to the rising stars who will redefine the way we think about business, here are the leading minds and landmark ideas that have established the *Harvard Business Review* as required reading for ambitious business people in organizations around the globe.

Other books in the series:

Harvard Business Review on Brand Management

Harvard Business Review on Breakthrough Thinking

Harvard Business Review on Business and the Environment

Harvard Business Review on the Business Value of IT

Harvard Business Review on Change

Harvard Business Review on Corporate Strategy

Harvard Business Review on Crisis Management

Harvard Business Review on Effective Communication

Harvard Business Review on Entrepreneurship

Harvard Business Review on Knowledge Management

Harvard Business Review on Leadership

Harvard Business Review on Managing High-Tech Industries

Harvard Business Review on Managing People

Harvard Business Review on Managing Uncertainty

Harvard Business Review on Managing the Value Chain

Harvard Business Review on Measuring Corporate Performance

Harvard Business Review on Negotiation and Conflict Resolution

Harvard Business Review on Nonprofits

Harvard Business Review on Strategies for Growth

Harvard Business Review

ON

CORPORATE

GOVERNANCE

The *Harvard Business Review* articles in this collection are available as
individual reprints. Discounts apply to quantity purchases. For information and ordering, please contact Customer Service, Harvard Business
School Publishing, Boston, MA 02163. Telephone: (617) 783-7500 or
(800) 988-0886, 8 A.M. to 6 P.M. Eastern Time, Monday through Friday.
Fax: (617) 783-7555, 24 hours a day. E-mail: custserv@hbsp.harvard.edu.

Library of Congress Cataloging-in-Publication Data
Harvard business review on corporate governance.
      p.   cm. — (Harvard business review paperback series)
    Includes index.
    ISBN 1-57851-237-9 (alk. paper)
    1. Corporate governance.   2. Boards of directors.   3. Corpora-
tions.   I. Harvard business review.   II. Title: Corporate governance.
III. Series.
HD2741.H289 2000
658.4'2—dc21   99-28457
                                                  CIP

*The paper used in this publication meets the requirements of the Ameri-
can National Standard for Permanence of Paper for Publications and
Documents in Libraries and Archives Z39.48-1992.*

Contents

Harvard Business Review

ON

CORPORATE

GOVERNANCE

Crisis Prevention

How to Gear Up Your Board

WALTER J. SALMON

Executive Summary

TODAY'S CRITICS OF CORPORATE BOARDROOMS have plenty of ammunition. The two crucial responsibilities of boards—oversight of long-term company strategy and the selection, evaluation, and compensation of top management—were reduced to damage control during the 1980s. Walter Salmon, a longtime director, notes that while boards have improved since he began serving on them in 1961, they haven't kept pace with the need for real change.

Based on over 30 years of boardroom experience, Salmon recommends against government reform of board practices. But he does prescribe a series of incremental changes as a remedy. To begin with, he suggests limiting the size of boards and increasing the number of outside directors on them. In fact, according to Salmon, only thee insiders belong on a board: the CEO, the COO, and the CFO.

1

Changing how committees function is also necessary for gearing up today's boards. The audit committee, for example, can periodically review "high-exposure areas" of a business, perhaps helping to prevent embarrassing drops in future profits. Compensation committees can structure incentive compensation for executives to emphasize long-term rather than short-term performance. And nominating committees should be responsible for finding new, independent directors—not the CEO.

In general, boards as a whole must spot problems early and blow the whistle, exercising what Salmon calls, "constructive dissatisfaction." On a revitalized board, directors have enough confidence in the process to vigorously challenge one another, including the company's chief executive.

As ANOTHER PROXY SEASON APPROACHES, board members—and I include myself in this diagnosis—may feel a little queasy. I've served on more than my share of corporate boards over the past 30 years, and I've rarely found that "passive," "supine," or "fat, dumb, and comfortable" (just a sample of recent comments about boards) describe the directors I've worked with. However, critics of the boardroom have plenty of substantive ammunition, and we can no longer avoid the glaring evidence that too many corporate boards fail to do their jobs.

After serving on my share of boards, I've rarely found that "fat, dumb, and comfortable" describe the directors I've worked with.

The two crucial responsibilities of boards—oversight of long-term company strategy and the selection, evaluation, and compensation of top management—were reduced to damage control during the 1980s. Boards that had tolerated mediocre performance were forced to acquiesce to mergers, acquisitions, and restructurings financed with mountains of debt. And despite disappointing performance, CEO compensation has skyrocketed in a manner that, with hindsight, few of us would have chosen.

Yet boards *have* improved. When I began my service as a board member in 1961, management constituted a majority of most boards, and these insiders handpicked the outside members. But according to recent surveys, such as those conducted by consulting groups like Korn/Ferry Organizational Consulting in Boston, the average board now consists of roughly nine outside directors and three inside directors. This is a significant improvement since the mid-1970s, when membership averaged five insiders and only eight outsiders.

Directors today receive more information, demand more justification for managerial decisions, and take their roles more seriously. In recent months, we've seen the board of GM actively intervene, the Sears board respond positively to shareholder suggestions, and the board of DEC deal decisively with CEO succession.

Still, many of us who serve on boards recognize that such improvements haven't kept pace with the need for real change. While some critics have argued that the government should legislate board reform, I believe that is both inadvisable and unnecessary. There are still many unexploited opportunities for boards to improve corporate performance rather than simply confining themselves to mopping up after disasters. As a long-time member of many boards, I can recommend a series of changes—and the right questions to ask when diagnosing board size, committee responsibilities, and how the board conducts its business. (See "22 Questions for Diagnosing Your Board" at the end of this article.)

The overall goal, of course, is what we all want: boards with a more open, constructive atmosphere, in which directors have enough confidence in the process to vigorously challenge each other. Better ongoing diagnosis, both by individual directors and the board as a whole, should vastly improve the chances of providing effective—and healthy—oversight of the companies we serve.

Board Size and Shape: Who's in Control?

Although the balance between insiders and outsiders has improved since the 1970s, many boards, particularly those of small, regional companies, continue to be over-populated with members of management.

This uneven balance of power, an all-too-common dynamic, may reveal a board that isn't functioning as it should. Inside directors are often too committed to tradition and their own ideas. Outside directors, without independent sources of information, are usually only capable of anemic discussion and dissent. The result: consumers, competition, technology, and the economy may all change, but the company fails to keep up.

In fact, only three insiders belong on boards: the CEO, the COO, and the CFO. As the current leaders of the corporation, the CEO and COO are there to communicate, explain, and justify strategic direction to the outside directors. Because the CFO shares fiduciary responsibility with the directors for both the quality of the numbers and the financial conduct of the corporation, he or she should also have a seat. In smaller companies, however, the CFO might attend board meetings and provide information without voting.

Although insiders such as the general counsel and the head of a function or division can provide invaluable information about their particular activities, they will understandably champion a more provincial point of view than that required of overseers of the whole corporation. I've served on a board where the presence of a division head inhibited other directors from candidly evaluating that division's disappointing performance. The board should have decided to restrict the unit's access to capital and human resources, for example, but did not because the division head was present.

Some people argue that additional members of management should be included on boards in order to acquaint outside directors with a cross-section of senior personnel. This is a worthy goal, but I have a better idea. In my experience, most connections between board members and senior managers are initiated by CEOs. If a director is interested in a particular operation, the CEO says, "You and Joe should talk." Most directors would hesitate, appropriately enough, to contact a manager without the CEO's sanction for fear of undermining his or her authority. But I suggest that CEOs encourage board members to meet with senior officers as a matter of course. Doing it away from the press of board meetings accomplishes two things: it increases the likelihood that a real relationship will develop and also that useful information will pass hands.

As for overall board size, between 8 and 15 members for large, publicly held companies is probably about right. Fewer than 8 directors cannot staff audit, compensation, and other committees with enough outside directors. But more than 15 members almost always diffuses and cuts into productive debate, since few board meetings last longer than four hours.

Board Committees: Can You Shift Responsibilities?

Of course, a sensible size and limited number of insiders are not the only important ingredients in establishing an effective board. Changing how committees function is also necessary for any board treatment plan to work.

The audit committee, for example, could add several responsibilities to its traditional agenda. In order to encourage the outside accountants to report potential threats to a company's health before they're cited as illegal practices or violations of accounting standards, the audit committee should displace management as the authority for approving the partner in charge of the job. Making the audit committee responsible for approving the presiding partner serves as a powerful reminder to the accounting firm that audit committee oversight means more than perfunctory consent to accounting policies and decisions.

The audit committee can contribute further to corporate performance by making a practice of periodically reviewing so-called "high-exposure areas," procedures under stress because of changes in the external business environment. For example, since off-price promotions have increased dramatically in the consumer packaged goods industry, it's much harder for manufacturers to estimate their receivables accurately. Audit committee oversight of the area could help ensure that reserves for possible future losses are high enough and thus prevent an embarrassing decline in future profits.

In addition, compensation committees could certainly take on more responsibility. Current compensation committees usually occupy themselves with how
much top management should be paid, the proportion
represented by salary, and the formulas used to govern
short-term and long-term incentives like stock options.
Yet there are many ways to perform these duties more
effectively. To begin with, when compensation consultants are hired—and they almost always are—the
board's compensation committee and not the company's
human resources officer should be their client. The consultants would then be less likely to make recommendations that favor top management.

Most compensation committees also focus primarily
on peer-group comparisons to ensure that the pay of top
executives is at least on a par with competitors. However, using peer-group comparisons often means staying
in line with the proportion of salary and short-term and
long-term incentives paid by the competition. In effect,
this focus abandons compensation as a means of placing
more weight on a company's long-term performance
than on competition. By tacitly reinforcing the emphasis
on short-term results, current compensation committees
fall into a trap that is both detrimental to the company
and the U.S. economy as a whole. But they don't have to.
It is definitely within this committee's power to structure
incentive compensation to emphasize long-term rather
than short-term performance.

What about the executive committee? By now, experienced directors may be wondering why I recommend
augmented roles for audit and compensation committees (to say nothing of nominating committees) but not
the executive. The reason is that executive committees
with too much muscle, by encouraging the emergence of

two-tier boards, are obstacles rather than aids to better corporate governance. In essence, directors on the executive committee become the "first tier," dominating decision making, while the role of the "second tier" directors is, like that of the House of Lords, reduced to giving advice and consent.

Some people argue that a powerful executive committee is necessary to handle serious emergencies between board meetings. However, jet travel, fax machines, and the availability of instant global communication make this argument obsolete. The authority of the executive committee should be limited to executing decisions that have been informally agreed upon by the full board. Actions like voting dividends in accordance with established policy or signing a sales agreement that the board has already endorsed fall within the limited—and reasonable—domain of this committee.

Performance Reviews: Who Evaluates Your CEO?

Few boards today conduct an annual review of the company's succession plans for senior management. Yet this is another duty more compensation committees should spearhead. Well-directed succession planning means thinking through the evolution of the company's organizational structure, the potential of current senior managers, and the actions required to satisfy future management needs. Although directors often talk informally about succession, making it a routine part of the annual agenda should stimulate actions that ultimately satisfy future management needs.

The logical climax of the compensation committee's involvement in succession planning is the annual evaluation of the CEO. This process should involve a dialogue with the chief executive about his or her strengths, weaknesses, objectives, personal plans, and, of course, performance. Evaluations provide constructive criticism of the CEO's performance—criticism only the compensation committee and outside directors have the authority to give.

The need to conduct such CEO evaluations was brought home to me in the case of one chief executive who focused far too much attention on earnings per share each quarter at the expense of the company's long-term health. Although earnings per share were inching up, other key barometers of corporate health like sales and asset turnover were below plan. Several of us on the board mentioned our concerns, but it was easy for the CEO to dismiss the suggestions of individual directors because there was no annual review during which he might have learned that we were all worried. In this case, a fine person and an essentially able CEO was forced to resign from a post that he might have retained had evaluation been a board ritual.

Evaluating the CEO also helps to preserve his or her humility, a trait that's hard to come by if you're the unchallenged leader of a sizable corporate entity. In addition, annual evaluations may encourage CEOs to appraise their own subordinates more thoroughly. Finally, if the evaluation is done prior to the annual review of the CEO's salary, the touchy compensation review process becomes more objective.

How does a board inaugurate formal evaluation? One of the best ways I can think of comes from the directors of a supermarket chain on whose board I serve: we established the CEO review when the company was doing well under an able chief executive. He wanted to set a precedent that would be good for him, his successor, the company, and—upon this CEO's retirement—the stock he intended to keep in the supermarket chain.

Because of its importance, a CEO's performance review, while orchestrated by the compensation committee, must involve all outside directors. The compensation committee can gather and synthesize the comments of other outside members and communicate them to the CEO, but the chief executive should still respond to this critique at a meeting attended by all outside directors.

Nominations: What's the Right Process?

From where I sit, vesting a board's nominating committee with the responsibility for finding new directors represents another healthy shift of authority. Yet this rarely happens in real life. Although half of the companies listed on the New York Stock Exchange have nominating committees, 89% of those surveyed by Korn/Ferry still depend on the recommendations of the chairman—in many cases the CEO—to select board members.

The job of finding new members should never be delegated to the CEO. Some chief executives select directors they "can count on" rather than individuals who constructively examine important issues. Often these individuals, the CEO, and other board members live and socialize in the same community. Fear of doing damage to social relationships can then deprive the CEO of necessary counsel, criticism, and performance assessment.

Of course, the CEO's input shouldn't be excluded. He or she should have good ideas about what skills are needed to serve on the board. And it's essential that the chief executive meet a prospective director before nomination, both to secure the CEO's support and to determine the candidate's willingness to serve on the board. But to symbolize who really has the authority to nominate directors, the chairman of the nominating committee, not the CEO, should extend the invitation to stand for election. Similarly, the authority for making committee assignments should also belong to the nominating committee to avoid, once again, the accusation that key committees like compensation—and the outside directors who serve on them—have been handpicked by the chief executive.

Clearly, outside directors with reputations for independence stand the best chance of adequately monitoring management. The practical problem lies in discovering who is really disinterested, able, and committed.

The word "disinterested" immediately disqualifies vendors of professional services like lawyers, bankers, and consultants. Their services and counsel can be obtained without board membership, and including them almost always inhibits frank assessment of their own firm's contribution. Their presence on the board also discourages competing providers from soliciting business, depriving the corporation of innovative ideas or lower prices.

Suppliers should be disqualified too, for the same reasons. However, representatives of important customers raise a more difficult issue. While they may provide unusual insights into the efficacy of the company's marketing efforts other customers may suspect that the customer-directors receive favorable treatment. In addition, when policies considered by the board would adversely affect the customer-director's own company, conflicts of interest sometimes arise. For example, recently we've heard of the problems encountered by banks when making loans to their own directors.

Disqualifying prospective board members, unfortunately, is much easier than figuring out who the ideal director might be. At the very least, the nominating committee must formulate criteria for candidates that include professional expertise, availability, age—and, possibly, sex, race, and nationality. After forming a list of requirements and qualifications, members of this committee should regularly solicit the rest of the board, including the CEO, for candidates. In addition, various organizations like Catalyst in New York offer lists of independent directors, and many boards now use professional search firms.

In general, personal attributes like integrity and the ability to listen with an open mind are essential requirements for good board members. Equally important, however, are the willingness to engage in constructive discussion with other board members and the fortitude to make tough decisions.

Directors who can speak their minds add substance and richness to board decisions. Companies don't need board members who convey their opinions only in private to the CEO. Such individuals end up converting a participatory environment into one in which decisions are an outcome of a mysterious series of unreconciled, one-on-one discussions.

Companies *do* need board members with backgrounds and skills that complement each other and are related to the mission of the particular corporation. For example, a retailer's board should include people with interests in marketing, management information systems and logistics, human resources, finance, real estate, and perhaps consumer lifestyles. Still, a good board is not just a collection of specialists; it is a group of thoughtful individuals who can counsel, support, and occasionally disagree with the CEO.

Having independent directors who can make tough decisions is important precisely because of the tough environment most boards find themselves in today. Board members may have to endure heated criticism for liquidating irreversibly marginal or uneconomic businesses despite the adverse effects on individuals and the community. And terminating the services of a no longer effective CEO with whom some board members may have developed a friendship is traumatic but sometimes necessary.

Board Business: Do All Directors Have a Say?

In most U.S. corporations, establishing the agenda and distributing materials are the responsibilities of the chairman, who is usually the CEO. While most CEO-chairmen undoubtedly do their best to focus the agenda on critical issues, their selection of meeting topics may not represent what outside board members have on their minds.

When a board chairman is also the CEO, a difference of opinion over what constitutes the critical issues may fail to surface. An outside director, unwilling to show a lack of confidence in the CEO, often feels awkward voicing concerns about the agenda. Although such diffidence should not interfere with frank discussion, in my experience it frequently does.

The solution advocated by Harvard Professor Jay Lorsch and others is to separate the roles of CEO and chairman. Although I have no objection to this idea, I think a more realistic solution to the problem of agenda-setting lies in assigning an outside director the task of helping the chairman plan the meeting's topics. This director could act as a conduit through which outsiders, without hesitation, raise issues they feel deserve board consideration.

While a thoughtful agenda provides a framework for constructive meetings, all directors need to know what's really going on in order to conduct board business effectively. In 1987, the directors who finally engineered the resignation of Mellon Bank's CEO, J. David Barnes, claimed they didn't act sooner because they never received adequate information about the bank's financial problems. As it happens, the board met only four times in 1985 and five times in 1986. To prevent such an information block, directors must make sure that enough relevant background material is distributed to the board in time to be digested before every meeting.

Two kinds of information help to make outside directors full partners in board discussions: routine data that show how well the company is doing against plan, competition, and the previous year's numbers; and specific facts that relate to the main agenda items for the next meeting. In addition, financial and performance data should be sent to directors monthly (even if they meet less frequently) so the board can stay on top of operations. Here's the information I've found most useful:

- operating statements, balance sheets, and statements of cash flow that compare current period and year-to-date numbers with the corporate plan and the previous year;

- management briefs that explain variations of the above from plan, including a revised forecast for the rest of the year;

- market-share figures;

- minutes of management committee meetings in which key reports were presented or capital expenditure actions taken;

- important news articles about the company and its competition;

- reports from financial analysts about the company and its competition.

For important discussions that demand a thorough debate of various courses of action, management should send a memorandum to all directors that defines the problem, presents the alternatives, and analyzes the probable financial and intangible consequences of pursuing each one. The memo ought to include best, worst, and most likely numbers—and conclude with management's recommendations, including acknowledgment of risk. For example, would a worst-case scenario jeopardize other initiatives, the dividend, or possibly lead to insolvency? Outside directors must receive this sort of analysis in time to make telephone calls for clarification or to obtain more facts before the meeting rather than relying only on what management initially sent them.

In addition to making sure information is distributed freely and in a timely fashion, directors may decide to hold longer meetings less frequently. Longer meetings not only allow more time for thoughtful discussion but also decrease travel time for busy executives. For example, many boards would do better with six long meetings a year rather than 12 short ones.

Of course, big boards, which often have no more than six meetings a year, suffer from their own particular afflictions. For one thing, chances are that their outside members don't know each other well. They fail to develop confidence and trust in each other and a resulting sense of cohesiveness. For that reason alone, I believe it's imperative that outside directors meet from time to time without management. For example, I'm on a board that routinely plans executive committee sessions right after the general board meetings. Without raising a threatening red flag in front of management, the occasion allows us to ask each other if what inside members said made sense.

When the chief executive is part of a company's problem, directors may resort to conferring surreptitiously. One such experience was enough to convince me of the importance of establishing mechanisms for early exposure and correction of problems, such as separate and planned meeting times for outside directors.

Planning and CEO Selection: Is Your Board in Charge?

While what I've discussed so far should enhance board effectiveness in general, two exceptionally important matters require special attention: participation in the long-range business plan and domination of the CEO selection process.

Stockholders should not expect a board to run a company on a daily basis, but they have a right to expect sufficient board involvement in long-range planning. Obviously, a responsible board must do more than listen to management's strategies and endorse them. When a board's involvement in long-range planning is too cursory, directors and management can't have a fruitful discussion about business strategies. Because the planning process itself almost always involves months of intense work, management is usually psychologically committed to the plan by the time of its presentation to the board. Under these circumstances, the board's discussion is typically lukewarm, followed by inadequately informed endorsement.

Responsible, effective boards participate in the long-range planning process right from the start by specifying the issues management should tackle. Then, if outside directors have had input from the beginning, their debate with management about the results will be more challenging and to the point. In addition, management is more likely to view the board as a partner in the planning process and thus will be less resistant to strategy changes directors may suggest.

As for CEO selection, if the board doesn't dominate the process, the incumbent chief executive certainly will. And, naturally enough, the incumbent will want to ordain a successor in his or her own image. Meanwhile, directors may know full well that changes in the business environment, the long-range plan, or the organization itself require a CEO with a completely new set of strengths. The board, therefore, has an inescapable obligation to head the search.

Human nature being what it is, directors don't ask themselves every year, "Do we need a new CEO?" If they do, then the board and the company have a problem. However, a CEO may choose to retire, or he or she may need to do so for reasons of poor health, other business commitments, or sometimes consistently poor performance. Under such special circumstances, boards must define the talents the next CEO should have, conduct the search (whether internally or externally), and finally appoint the best available candidate. Although directors should seriously consider the opinions of the current chief executive and, for that matter, senior managers, the board must ultimately select the new CEO.

Active Directors: What's the Payoff?

Assuming no unexpected crises, active board service, including preparation, takes up to $2^1/_2$ times the number of hours spent at meetings. So if, ideally, a board and its committees meet six times a year for an average length of six hours, board business occupies from 9 to $11^1/_4$ days of an individual director's year.

The prescription I've set forth won't work without committed directors, both in the number of hours they spend on the job and their overall focus of attention. Although the main returns of active board service are emotional and intellectual, as well as the insights that can be carried over to other professional activities, pay is obviously another motivating factor.

For public companies, total director compensation averages $33,133, according to Korn/Ferry's latest survey. At the higher end—say, $50,000 to $60,000—the figures represent reasonable remuneration based on the opportunity cost of most directors. However, the current forms of compensation typically do not integrate directors' pay with their performance. As a result, more companies are offering directors restricted stock or stock options in addition to or in lieu of retainers and meeting fees.

But if performance-oriented pay is the order of the day, those who set directors' compensation—generally the board itself—must decide over what time period to measure that performance. Since the basic mission of directors is to protect the company's long-term health and to ensure its survival, performance pay should also be oriented toward the long term. I'd say a five-year period before stock restrictions lapse or options can be exercised is a sensible horizon for directors. Performance pay also ought to be contingent on a threshold level of corporate performance.

Even if a company is fortunate enough to attract talented and dedicated people as directors, there's no assurance they'll remain so. If boards are to provide better governance, provisions must be made for the departure of directors who no longer pull their weight.

Rather than stipulating a mandatory retirement age for directors, Dayton-Hudson has adopted this approach: it limits length of service on the board to 12 years in order to encourage fresh thinking. Other companies have a policy that board members must submit a resignation if they change their principal employment on the grounds that a change of jobs could alter their suitability as directors. In such cases, the resignation is submitted to either the nominating committee or to all outside members, who then decide if asking the director to stay is in the company's interest. Although such a review of qualifications is better than no review at all, it takes an unpredictable event to trigger the process.

As with CEO evaluations, boards must institute periodic, formal reviews of directors. Outside directors, with management's input, can appraise the performance of each of their colleagues at, for example, five-year intervals after the first appointment. Based on such reviews, directors who aren't pulling their weight should not be nominated for reelection.

But at what point should a director whose opinions on important matters are ignored or consistently overruled resign? And if a director resigns, should he or she disclose the real reason or gloss it over with the usual refrain about the "press of other business"?

While directors cling as much as anyone else to the hope that their colleagues can be won over, there comes a time when remaining on a board with which you're in fundamental disagreement feels too uncomfortable. In addition, remaining on the board implies to other stockholders a consensus that doesn't really exist. Although circumstances may vary, most directors in this bind, including myself, would feel obliged to alert stockholders and others to the actual reasons for resignation.

Group Trust: Can Your Board Blow the Whistle?

I've recommended that companies must limit the number of insiders, control the size of the board, increase and shift responsibilities, and seek independent directors. These are all important elements of a good treatment plan, but in the end, it's the quality of group actions that will—or will not—enable a board to fulfill its mission. Sometimes a single voice does rise against the management of a company, as in the case of Roderick Hills of Oak Industries, who had his own ideas about corporate direction and ultimately ousted management. But boards can't rely on single voices to guarantee the long-term health of their companies.

Boards as a whole must be able to spot problems early and blow the whistle, exercising what I and others like to call "constructive dissatisfaction." Recently, the directors of one company I know exhibited constructive dissatisfaction at a time when the business seemed to be doing well. The company, a chain of fitness centers, was turning in consistently good profits. It seemed financially impregnable, with 99% equity, 1% debt. However, the directors noticed that in one small respect performance had declined: the number of clients who entered the facilities every day had dropped. The board confronted the CEO and suggested that instead of continuing to do what the company had previously done well, perhaps it was time to try something else—for example, a change in marketing strategy. In this case, the directors stimulated the CEO to bring in a consulting firm, which looked hard at established practices.

To stay on the alert, boards must take measures to build trust among members. Group trips to corporate facilities at a distance from headquarters can help. The CEO and outside directors of a board I'm on attend a dinner the night before board meetings to discuss matters that are "politically sensitive," such as the performance of senior managers. In this informal way, many issues have surfaced that probably wouldn't have arisen otherwise.

In any case, to say that a board can transform itself from a rubber stamp to an early warning system by altering any of the boardroom conditions I've mentioned would be an oversimplification. When a company goes into a tailspin, we know by implication that the board wasn't doing its job. But even astute observers usually can't pin the blame on one or even two or three mistakes. Just as malfunctioning boards rarely suffer from a single malady—allowing the CEO to pick new directors, for example—no single change will make directors more effective. Only by following a comprehensive treatment plan that addresses the sore points I've discussed can boards restore their good health.

22 Questions for Diagnosing Your Board

If you answer yes to all 22 questions, you have an exemplary board.

1. Are there three or more outside directors for every insider?

2. Are the insiders limited to the CEO, the COO, and the CFO?

3. Do your directors routinely speak to senior managers who are not represented on the board?

4. Is your board the right size (8 to 15 members)?

5. Does your audit committee, not management, have the authority to approve the partner in charge of auditing the company?

6. Does your audit committee routinely review "high-exposure" areas?

7. Do compensation consultants report to your compensation committee rather than to the company's human resources officers?

8. Has your compensation committee shown the courage to establish formulas for CEO compensation based on long-term results—even if the formulas differ from industry norms?

9. Are the activities of your executive committee sufficiently contained to prevent the emergence of a "two-tier" board?

10. Do outside directors annually review succession plans for senior management?

11. Do outside directors formally evaluate your CEO's strengths, weaknesses, objectives, personal plans, and performance every year?

12. Does your nominating committee rather than the CEO direct the search for new board members and invite candidates to stand for election?

13. Is there a way for outside directors to alter the meeting agenda set by your CEO?

14. Does the company help directors prepare for meetings by sending relevant routine information, as well as analyses of key agenda items, ahead of time?

15. Is there sufficient meeting time for thoughtful discussion in addition to management monologue?

16. Do the outside directors meet without management on a regular basis?

17. Is your board actively involved in formulating long-range business strategy from the start of the planning cycle?

18. Does your board, rather than the incumbent CEO, select the new chief executive—in fact as well as in theory?

19. Is at least some of directors' pay linked to corporate performance?

20. Is the performance of each of your directors periodically reviewed ?

21. Are directors who are no longer pulling their weight discouraged from standing for reelection?

22. Do you take the right measures to build trust among directors?

Originally published in January–February 1993
Reprint 93106

Empowering the Board

JAY W. LORSCH

Executive Summary

IF THE 1980S WERE THE DECADE when the movement to empower U.S. factory and office workers took
root, the 1990s are the decade when empowerment is
sweeping corporate boardrooms. Empowerment means
that outside directors have the capability and independence to monitor the performance of top management
and the company; to influence management to change
the strategic direction of the company if its performance
does not meet the board's expectations; and, in the most
extreme cases, to change corporate leadership.

Because the chief executive is also the board chair in
more the 80% of the country's publicly held corporations,
most CEOs view board empowerment with trepidation.
But, Jay Lorsch argues, if CEOs resist the trend, they and
their companies will be the losers because the empowered board is here to stay. If CEOs recognize that

empowered directors can help them and their companies, board empowerment can be achieved with minimal fuss and maximum benefit to CEOs, shareholders, and the U.S. economy.

This rosy scenario, however, means that outside directors and the CEO must redefine their relationship. The CEO must understand the power and the responsibility of the board, and outside directors must recognize and respect the boundary between monitoring management and actually managing the company. What is required is a new form of teamwork in which directors and senior managers understand one another's roles and collaborate effectively to achieve corporate success. Their newly defined relationship will strengthen the board's ability to advise management and to monitor corporate performance. The CEO will retain the power to lead the company while obtaining the guidance of informed and active directors as long as corporate performance is satisfactory.

I f   t h e   1 9 8 0 s   w e r e the decade when the movement to empower U.S. factory and office workers took root, the 1990s are the decade when empowerment is sweeping corporate boardrooms. Empowerment means that outside directors have the capability and independence to monitor the performance of top management and the company; to influence management to change the strategic direction of the company if its performance does not meet the board's expectations; and, in the most extreme cases, to change corporate leadership.

Because the chief executive is also the board chair in more than 80% of the country's publicly held corporations, it is not surprising that most chief executives view board empowerment with trepidation. Traditionally, corporate leaders have considered a powerful, active board to be a nuisance at best and a force that could improperly interfere in the management of the company at worst. They have preferred directors who are content to offer counsel when asked and to support management in times of crisis.

Chief executives who resist empowered boards must change their attitude. If they do not, they and their companies will be the losers because the empowered board is here to stay. If CEOs resist the trend, pressures to empower directors are likely to grow outside the boardroom, which will make the change adversarial and may lead to boardroom practices that *will* interfere unduly with management. But if CEOs recognize that empowered directors can help them and their companies, and if they encourage this trend, board empowerment can be achieved with minimal fuss and maximum benefit to CEOs, shareholders, and the U.S. economy.

This rosy scenario, however, means that outside directors and the chief executive must redefine their relationship. The CEO must understand clearly the power and responsibility of the board. Outside directors must recognize and respect the boundary between monitoring management and actually managing the company. What is required is a new form of teamwork in which directors and top-level managers understand one another's roles and responsibilities and collaborate effectively to achieve corporate success. Their newly defined relationship will strengthen the board's ability to advise management and to monitor corporate performance. The CEO will retain the power to lead the company while obtaining the guidance of informed and active directors as long as corporate performance is satisfactory.

Pressures for Empowerment

There are several driving forces to empower outside directors. First, most institutional investors do not want to sit on boards and play a direct role in governing companies, but they have become more willing to pressure boards to challenge management and have been effective in getting the media to do the same. Recently, representatives of union pension funds, such as the Teamsters, have joined the ranks of shareholder activists. And changes in Securities and Exchange Commission regulations that make it easier for institutional shareholders to communicate with one another about corporate governance issues have increased the clout of those shareholders.

Second, the recent performance difficulties of many major companies and the removal of their CEOs have generated more public interest in active boards. Third, government competitiveness councils have stressed the link between corporate governance and competitive success, as has Chancellor William T. Allen of the Delaware Court of Chancery, in whose state more than half of U.S. public companies are incorporated.

Finally, the move to empower directors has been fueled by the controversy about CEO compensation—or, more precisely, by the perception that many CEOs are substantially overpaid relative to their companies' performance. Richard C. Breeden, who was chairman of the SEC from 1989 to 1993, believed that one way of tackling the issue was to make outside directors more accountable for top managers' pay. To that end, he and his fellow commissioners required companies to provide more details in their proxies about executive compensation, including how it was determined and how it related to the company's performance.

Several organizations have led the way in empowering their boards. (See the exhibit "The Progress of Board Empowerment.") Most of them—including Campbell Soup Company, Mallinckrodt, and Stanhome—have

---

The Progress of Board Empowerment

Company	Innovation
Dayton Hudson Corporation	Requires the outside directors to conduct an annual evaluation of the CEO.
Medtronic	Solicits opinions on board procedures by requiring all directors to complete a questionnaire; then the full board reviews the results at an annual meeting and tries to make improvements.
Stanhome	Developed a formal document that specifies the board's purpose, size, proportion of outside directors, annual calendar, and expectations of directors and management.
Mallinckrodt	Separated the roles of chair and CEO.
Lukens	Formed a committee of outside directors to study a major acquisition proposal, hold discussions with management, and recommend action to the full board.
Campbell Soup Company	Designated a lead director with the title of vice chairman.
Monsanto	Increased the proportion of the board's time that would be focused on stategic direction and considered specific capital proposals within that framework.
General Motors	Developed an explicit set of guidelines that outline how the board will function and be structured.

Note: The companies are listed in the chronological order in which they made significant moves toward empowerment. The innovation listed is only one of several changes each board has made. Members of the American Society of Corporate Secretaries provided some of these examples.

done so not because of outside pressure or poor company performance but because they believed it was the right thing to do. But too many CEOs still seem to view calls for board empowerment with alarm.

Invalid Assumptions About Empowering Directors

Many CEOs and others with reservations about empowering outside directors proceed from incorrect premises about power and the boardroom.

Power is zero-sum.   This is a serious misconception. As U.S. factories and offices illustrate, one party (employees) can gain power without the other party (management) losing it. The same is true in the boardroom. In companies such as Dayton Hudson Corporation and Medtronic, where directors have long been empowered to monitor corporate and management performance, there is no evidence that the CEO and other top-level managers have found their power to lead the company diminished. What they have found is that directors are better informed, communicate their ideas more effectively, and in general provide better advice. For example, at the steel company Lukens, the chairman and CEO asked several outside directors to serve on a board committee to consider a major acquisition in great detail. Each director reviewed all the data used by management to recommend the acquisition, and then the committee met for a daylong session with the management team. In the end, the committee recommended the acquisition to the full board, which approved it with understanding

In companies where directors are empowered, CEOs do not find their power diminished.

and enthusiasm. The CEO commented that as a result of the process, the full board had become more active, involved, and communicative and that the change in procedure had been valuable.

Advising and monitoring are in conflict. Advice is what CEOs want most from outside directors, and many chief executives worry that if directors become more forceful monitors, their usefulness as advisers will diminish. That concern is misguided because directors require the same two ingredients to perform both roles: access to useful information and the time to discuss it with one another and with management. In fact, directors on empowered boards are likely to be more knowledgeable and involved than those on traditional boards and therefore to be better advisers. It is true, of course, that if top management consistently disregards the directors' advice, an empowered board is more likely to be forceful in expressing its opinions. While such forthrightness may be uncomfortable to managers at first, it should lead to better decisions if directors and managers are working together effectively.

There is no need to act unless a crisis strikes. The assumption that boards can safely remain passive until there is a crisis implies that directors are like firefighters who sit around the station playing checkers until there is a fire and then spring into action. Firefighters must practice in order to cope with an emergency, and so must directors. Directors who passively await a crisis will have neither the necessary information nor the decision-making and communication mechanisms they need to resolve issues quickly if one does strike.

Moreover, as the events at such companies as General Motors and IBM have illustrated, the most difficult crises confronting boards occur gradually. Boards that do not actively monitor performance, even in apparently good times, are likely to have great difficulty spotting and understanding problems in a timely fashion. An important virtue of board empowerment is that it enables directors to prevent crises. By being active monitors, they can encourage and support their CEO in making the changes necessary to keep small difficulties from turning into large ones. In fact, in organizations whose boards removed CEOs because of poor corporate performance, the boards themselves usually had failed to monitor management and company performance in the years before the crisis.

One size fits all companies. Many managers incorrectly assume that empowerment should entail identical procedures and processes in all boards. While there are certain essential activities in which any board should engage—as I will explain below—the specifics of how the board should carry out those activities and, more broadly, act as advisers and monitors must depend on the company's particular circumstances.

At least three factors influence the processes and procedures that outside directors should use. First is the confidence the directors have in the CEO and the nature of the relationship between them. If the CEO is new and the directors do not have a good understanding of his or her ideas, they may want to monitor those ideas and the CEO's actions more frequently and carefully. If the CEO has been leading the company successfully for several years, directors can be effective monitors

The board's role as monitor will depend on the complexity of the decisions facing managers.

with less detailed, annual assessments. In the latter situation, however, outside directors must satisfy themselves that neither they nor the CEO is overlooking significant changes in the circumstances facing the company.

A second factor that affects the way a board should think about empowerment is the company's performance. If a company has been having problems, the directors will clearly want to be more involved in understanding management's thinking and decisions than if the company has not. Again, at the least, the directors should feel sure that they and management are anticipating the future and not overlooking potential problems.

The board's role as monitor will also depend on the complexity of the decisions facing managers and directors. Beyond problems with company performance, the factor that most influences such complexity is the diversity of the company's businesses—in other words, the number of different products and markets and also the number of countries in which the company operates. For example, the board of a company such as Procter & Gamble, which operates different businesses all over the world, has more complexity to deal with than the board of Lukens, which basically is in only one business and operates in only one country.

Some would argue that a company's size is also a determinant of the complexity of the decisions it faces. While that argument has some merit, size alone has less of an effect on complexity than diversity does. In essence, a bigger company has to make bigger decisions about the same issues, but if a company engages in a greater number of businesses, that means more and *different* issues for the board.

Another factor that affects the complexity of decisions is the rate of market and technological change in the company's businesses. Clearly, a company such as IBM, which not only has multiple businesses operating globally but also deals with constant and rapid technological and market changes, faces immense complexity. The task of keeping abreast of those changes is enormous.

Complexity as determined by such factors presents a serious challenge. The more complexity a company faces, the more difficult it is for directors to be effective monitors, because they constantly must be alert to changes, especially ones that are hard to anticipate.

What monitoring involves in a given company will change over time, as conditions change. Directors must have the information they need to focus on the right issues and use their time together productively. The effectiveness of the group is the true source of their empowerment. To understand why, let's consider the sources and limits of outside directors' power.

The Sources and Limits of Directors' Power

In theory, the directors' mandate to govern a company comes from the laws of the state in which it is incorporated. To the layman, those definitions of the board's role are surprisingly vague and broad. For example, according to Delaware law, "The business and affairs of every corporation organized under this charter shall be managed by or under the direction of a board of directors." Directors usually delegate the responsibility of operating the company to management. In carrying out their residual responsibility of overseeing management, they are expected to demonstrate care and loyalty (have no conflicts of interest) and to exercise business judgment. Laws defining directors' powers in other states generally follow those of Delaware.

Of course, these broad duties have been interpreted and refined by court decisions in the individual states and especially in Delaware. In addition, the stock exchanges and the Securities and Exchange Commission have developed rules and regulations that further define directors' duties. For example, the exchanges require audit committees to be composed of outside directors, and the SEC has prescribed how compensation committees should report top management's pay to shareholders.

While such actions enhance a board's ability to govern, the broader legal framework really does little more than provide a board with legitimacy to govern. Its real power and ability depend on two other sources: the knowledge that directors have and their cohesion as a group. Each source must be considered in relation to the CEO, because a board's real power depends on its relationship with the CEO and with other top executives.

One important factor is that directors are part-timers and the CEO is a full-time employee whose entire career may have been with the company. Not surprisingly, CEOs have knowledge about their companies that directors do not. From the directors' perspective, it is not an exaggeration to say that a primary purpose of board meetings is to learn about the organization from the CEO. Directors may obtain any data they want, but such information must be converted into useful

Given the experience and ability of directors on most boards, only a stubborn and arrogant CEO would resist a unified board.

knowledge through the prism of a broader understanding of the company and its markets and operations— information that inevitably must come from management at board meetings. The financial and written data tell only part of the story, and directors usually come to meetings armed with many questions: Why are revenues up or down? What are customers and dealers doing? Why are manufacturing costs declining? What is the status of a new product in a test market? Why are negotiations on a proposed acquisition taking so long?

Superior knowledge about such matters provides even the most well-intentioned CEO with a real power advantage over the outside directors. If we add to this advantage the fact that the CEO usually determines the board's agenda and leads its meetings, it is clear why CEOs must be convinced of the value of empowered directors. If they resist the idea, they can easily inhibit progress.

Directors, however, have a critical source of power that they can use to their advantage: their solidarity as a group. Given the experience and ability of the directors on most boards, only a stubborn and arrogant CEO would resist a unified board. As we have seen in the past few years, when a united board decides that it's time for a change in corporate direction or leadership, it prevails. Previously, the process of building such consensus may have taken too long because boardroom norms inhibited directors from communicating freely with one another. An empowered board, however, can facilitate the necessary dialogue and build solidarity among its members.

What Makes an Empowered Board?

Much has been said and written lately about the characteristics of an empowered board. These characteristics, which are being adopted to varying degrees in different boardrooms, can be summarized as follows:

- Most of the directors come from outside the company and have no other relationship with it.

- The board is small enough to be a cohesive group. Its members understand their common objectives and are willing to dedicate the time to accomplish them. They recognize that their primary obligation is to monitor the company's management and performance, not to manage the company.

- Members represent a range of business and leadership experiences, which are pertinent to understanding the issues the company faces.

- Members communicate freely with one another in both committee meetings and board meetings and outside such settings—with and without management.

- If the CEO is also chair of the board, the outside directors select a leader from among themselves. This person leads their deliberations when they meet without management and works closely with the CEO to plan board activities.

- Committees are made up entirely of outside directors. While management is consulted on matters discussed within the committees, they also meet regularly without management.

- Members receive information about the company's financial and product-market performance in a format that is intelligible and enables them to understand their company's performance relative to the competition's.

Such characteristics are the foundation on which board empowerment is being built, but the critical and less explored issues are what empowered boards should do differently as they monitor and advise, and how they should carry out their activities without interfering with management's duty and capacity to run the company.

Three activities are crucial if the board is to be an effective monitor: ensuring legal and ethical conduct by the corporation's officers and employees; approving the company's strategic direction and evaluating its progress; selecting, evaluating, rewarding, and if necessary removing the CEO, and ensuring that appropriate top-management succession plans are in place.

For years, directors have identified those three activities as their most important responsibilities. The first is the one with the longest history and the one that is accomplished most uniformly across the broad spectrum of U.S. companies. Audit committees made up of outside directors in all public companies ensure that financial reports are accurate, that accounting rules are followed, and that assets are not misappropriated. Many audit committees also review officers' and employees' compliance with other rules and standards of conduct. While some boards have failed in handling this responsibility, most notably in some commercial banks and in the savings and loan industry, this is not generally an area that needs substantial improvement.

Empowered boards should not interfere with management's capacity to run the company.

To monitor effectively, boards must also use their greater power to review and approve corporate strategy and to evaluate CEO performance and succession planning at least annually. A brief review of how most boards have been carrying out those two responsibilities will illustrate why they are the areas requiring the greatest change.

Traditionally, boards become involved in thinking about strategic direction when they approve specific capital or acquisition proposals. During the past decade, in a growing number of companies, boards have held one- or two-day strategic retreats. While that development is commendable, what happens at the retreats varies considerably. In some companies—for example, General Mills—managers inform directors of their intended strategy either through briefing books provided in advance or through oral presentations made at the retreat. Directors share their reactions and concerns at the retreat or later in private discussions with the CEO. Alternatively—for example, at AT&T—strategic retreats have been used for directors and senior officers to have an open, no-holds-barred discussion of changes in their industry.

At AT&T, directors and senior officers use strategic retreats for no-holds-barred discussions of changes in their industry.

While such approaches to involving board members represent an advance over the traditional practice of simply asking them to approve major projects individually, they do not go far enough. What is needed is for more boards to approve explicitly the strategic directions proposed by management and to review progress annually. Today only a few leading-edge boards take that approach.

The practice of evaluating the CEO realistically has also, until recently, been restricted to a few companies. The acknowledged pioneer has been Dayton Hudson Corporation, and its directors and managers have gradually spread the gospel around the Twin Cities and beyond—for example, to companies such as Hannaford

Brothers and Medtronic. Outside the Dayton Hudson orbit, a few other companies, such as Alcoa and Stanhome, have also developed explicit CEO reviews. But in most companies, the traditional practice has been a casual conversation between the chair of the compensation committee and the CEO about the latter's compensation and how it relates to his or her and the company's performance. More and more companies need a thorough evaluation process if the board's monitoring is to succeed.

A final aspect of the board's monitoring work is implementing a schedule of planning and review for the board and management. Such calendars guide meeting agendas in organizations like Dayton Hudson, Medtronic, and Stanhome. The calendars designate specific board meetings for strategic planning and review, for reviewing CEO performance, and for reviewing management succession plans. Not only do such schedules organize and focus the board's work, but they also emphasize for directors and management alike the interconnectedness of the key facets of the directors' role as monitors.

Effective Empowerment

While empowered directors have many concerns, they are now focusing much of their attention on CEO performance evaluation and corporate strategy. They hope that by doing a better job on these matters, they will avoid the problems that plagued many major companies in the past decade, when both directors and managers failed to recognize changes in technology and markets that adversely affected their companies.

Evaluating the CEO annually is central to effective monitoring for several reasons. Fundamentally, it is a major step toward empowering the board because it delivers a clear message to both the CEO and the directors that the former is accountable to the latter. It also provides outside directors with an impetus to engage in an open and frank discussion about the CEO's and the company's performances at least once a year. As a result, they will understand their company and its leader better and will be more effective monitors. A director who has served on two boards that have conducted CEO evaluations says that on most boards without careful CEO reviews, the outside directors don't have much opportunity to talk to one another. On the two boards with such evaluations, directors don't necessarily want to criticize the CEO, but they find it useful to converse openly about issues they may not want to bring up in front of the CEO. The director adds that such discussions allow directors to learn more about the organization and provide a forum for addressing concerns.

Finally, an evaluation benefits the CEO personally by directly communicating the directors' concerns and suggestions for improvement, as well as their praise. If it is done properly, it also allows the CEO to discuss his or her reactions with the directors. All corporate leaders realize that such feedback and dialogue are invaluable but all too rare.

As the list of companies whose boards evaluate the CEO has grown to include Alcoa, Brunswick, General Motors, Honeywell, and the St. Paul Companies, among others, unique approaches to such evaluations have been developed. However, certain criteria are essential to an effective evaluation:

- It should be conducted at least annually.

- It should assess the company's annual and long-term performance in comparison with that of similar organizations.

- The CEO's accomplishments should be judged against individual goals as well as against the goals for the company's performance. The CEO's individual goals should cover initiatives like starting a major quality-improvement program or making an acquisition. While such goals will vary from year to year, the CEO should continuously plan for top-management succession.

- The CEO should provide an assessment of his or her own performance.

- The outside directors should make their assessments individually. Their judgments should be combined by one director, a committee of directors, or an independent party so that they indicate the general tenor of the directors' assessments as well as the range of their views. This feedback should be transmitted to the CEO confidentially.

- The CEO should discuss the evaluation face-to-face with one or more outside directors and should have the opportunity to discuss his or her reactions to the review with all the directors.

Once a board and its CEO have implemented such a review, the roles of each party are quite clear. The CEO will set his or her objectives and do a self-appraisal, and the directors will assess and communicate how well they think the CEO is performing. Once the CEO and the board agree that such a process is desirable, there should be little dispute about the division of responsibility between CEOs and directors.

The related question of when and how deeply the board should become involved in strategic matters is less clear and likely to remain more controversial. A long-standing concern of both managers and directors is where to draw the line that separates management and board prerogatives. An outside director at Lukens who was actively involved in developing strategy said there is a fine line between having a director contribute ideas to the company's strategic direction and having that director try to manage the company.

There is a fine line between a director who contributes ideas to company strategy and one who tries to manage the company.

Once a director crosses that line, the board has real problems, because directors should not run the company. The director suggested that in such cases, maybe management should hold back information at board meetings.

Withholding information from the board is certainly not a good solution to the problem, but the question about where to draw the line is important. A senior executive at Lukens was clear about the distinction between directors and managers: "As each side moves closer to the dividing line, the responsibilities of each begin to look the same. But they are not the same, so the line needs to be drawn in such a way to ensure that managers manage and the board approves. You cannot have the whole group managing and approving together."

At a minimum, directors should approve corporate strategy and review and evaluate its results. How involved they should become in specific strategic decisions depends on specific circumstances. For example, at

Lukens, the chairman and CEO asked the committee of outside directors to become involved in an acquisition proposal because the decision was of great importance to the future of the company, whose performance had been lagging. Furthermore, the CEO was new and wanted to be certain that the directors supported the initiative. In such circumstances, it is prudent for directors to be more deeply involved in strategic decisions.

Even in companies that have established CEOs and are performing well, some decisions may be of such magnitude that management seeks or the board desires involvement. For example, at AT&T, the chairman and CEO held a strategic retreat with the board to discuss the impact of wireless communication on the company. The purpose of such informal meetings is for the CEO to get the directors' advice as well as to prepare the directors for a possible major decision. At AT&T, these discussions seem to have prepared the company for the McCaw acquisition more than a year later.

Just as democratic governments rule with the consent of the governed, so must boards.

While in both examples, management invited the board's involvement in strategy, the legal responsibility to determine where to draw the line between the board's monitoring and management's development and implementation of strategy belongs to the board. Monitoring will not work if directors and top management have not agreed about their respective roles. One of the tenets of American democracy has always been that the government rules with the consent of the governed. In a different sense, the same must be true as boards become empowered. Corporate leaders, who are the governed, must believe that the means the board has chosen to monitor strategy are reasonable and viable, and do not interfere with management's prerogatives. For that reason, both CEOs and directors must have a means of reviewing and adjusting the line between the board's and management's prerogatives. I shall return to this point, but first let's consider the major factor in how effective directors can be as monitors: the knowledge they need to carry out their activities.

Directors' Knowledge

To contribute effectively to discussions of corporate strategy and to evaluate CEO performance competently, directors obviously need adequate knowledge. *Knowledge* is the appropriate word here instead of the more frequently used *information* because the directors' real problem is not lack of information but its content and context. One director says that most boards spend too much time watching presentations when what they really need is to understand the material presented so they can participate more effectively. In the 1989 survey of boards for *Pawns or Potentates*, the book I coauthored with Elizabeth MacIver, and in subsequent interviews with many directors, very few directors expressed a concern about adequate information. Their real concern was having too much information to digest in the time they had available. Under the U.S. system of governance, outside directors are part-timers. No matter how diligent they want to be, there is a limit to how much time they can devote to a particular board.

Directors receive information in two ways. The first is written reports. Typically, they contain information about the company's financial results as well as about specific proposals to be discussed at a particular meeting. The second is oral presentations by managers; especially important is the CEO's report, which is a central feature of most board meetings. While the specific content may vary from one boardroom to another, the CEO's remarks about the state of the company and events affecting it since the previous meeting are an important source of knowledge for directors.

In general, directors absorbed all those data over many years of service and gradually converted them into knowledge about the company. In many boardrooms of the past, such a gradual approach to building knowledge was adequate. However, in companies faced with long-term decline because of rapidly changing market and technological conditions, this approach proved inadequate. Directors were no more aware

The challenge for directors is to turn a broad array of information into useful knowledge quickly.

of the significance of external events than were top-level managers. One reason for the myopia may have been that managers were the providers of information to the board. But another may have been that directors are long on financial knowledge and short on knowledge about changing markets and technology. It is not that management willfully withheld information about products and markets but that, traditionally, such data were not judged to be within the board's purview.

If boards are to be effective in evaluating the CEO and approving corporate strategy, they need to develop knowledge not only about the company's financial results, which are an indication of past performance, but also about the company's progress in accomplishing its strategy. That means understanding progress in developing new technology and new products and services, and in entering new markets. It means understanding changing customer requirements and what competitors are doing. Similarly, directors need the data to build knowledge about the organizational health of the company. In essence, they need their own version of the "balanced scorecard," which Robert S. Kaplan and David P. Norton recommend for managers in "Putting the Balanced Scorecard to Work" (HBR, September–October 1993).

As in other aspects of a board's work, directors and managers must decide what mix of knowledge is appropriate to the company's circumstances. Again, there are certain minimal requirements. The data must be balanced between financial and strategic issues and focused on future prospects as well as past performance. Information must be grounded in strategic objectives and competitive demands, and it must paint a broad picture of the conditions the company is facing. The data should also shed light on the CEO's progress toward achieving his or her individual goals.

The challenge for directors is to take what may be a greater quantity and a broader array of information and turn it into useful knowledge quickly. Some boards, such as Monsanto Company's, deal with this challenge by increasing the capital limits of projects requiring board approval, thus freeing up time to devote to broader strategic issues.

Another practice followed by Monsanto's and Alcoa's boards is to ask directors periodically for their assessment of the information they receive. This practice encourages directors to provide one another and management with an explicit review of information and discourages the company from supplying the same types of data because "we have always done it that way." Another solution to the problem of more information is to ensure that data are organized efficiently and provide a concise but comprehensive overview of the company's strategic progress. Data should be sent to the directors in advance so they can study them, formulate questions, and identify issues they would like to discuss at board meetings. Directors should have the option of meeting alone to develop their collective understanding of the company's situation and to decide which questions and issues they want to discuss with management. A growing number of boards—for example, Alcoa's, General Motors', and Medtronic's—are now doing that.

Such steps should enable directors to keep up with events in a rapidly changing world so they can make informed approvals of specific strategic issues and in-depth judgments about the CEO's accomplishments and goals. Those steps are essential to the board's role as an effective monitor.

Self-Monitoring

In this dynamic world, no set of board activities is likely to constitute effective monitoring for very long. Conditions facing the company will change, as will the membership of the board. The inevitability of change and the fact that even the most talented and well-motivated directors and managers will find that their best-laid plans do not always work mean that an empowered board must periodically monitor its own performance. Boards at AlliedSignal, General Motors, Honeywell, Medtronic, and Texaco already monitor themselves. At some companies, such as Medtronic, the outside directors use an annual questionnaire to solicit opinions from themselves and from managers, and then review the results of the survey to find opportunities for improvement. At other companies, directors simply devote part of a meeting, usually annually, to a discussion of how well the board has been conducting its affairs and how its performance can be improved.

The idea of the entire board's reviewing its own activities annually is sound because it enables all directors, both insiders and outsiders, to contribute their ideas for improvement and thus be committed to any changes in process. Regardless of the specific process used, how well a board is conducting its duties must be assessed in light of the conditions the directors are confronting: What is their relationship with the CEO, and how much confidence do they have in him or her? How well has the company been performing? How complex are the issues facing the directors?

In the context of the circumstances, directors need to assess how well they are understanding and monitoring the company's strategy. How well is the process of CEO evaluation working? How effectively do the directors use their time together? How well are board committees functioning? Are directors getting the appropriate information, and is it well organized? Those are some of the major concerns that should be addressed to make boards more effective monitors.

The review of procedures will be conducted most efficiently if the directors have designed in advance an explicit set of principles about how they intend to function as a board, as General Motors' board did in the company's 1994 guidelines. Creating such guidelines, while time consuming, causes directors to reason together about what changes they may want to make. Once such principles have been established, they also provide directors with a clear framework against which to judge their performance. In addition to reviewing their processes and procedures, a few boards are conducting explicit reviews of individual directors. For example, AlliedSignal has established a process whereby individual directors are reviewed at the time of their renomination.

This suggests that while the full board can be involved in both aspects of evaluation, the board's committees can also play a role in monitoring the board's work. The compensation committee can focus on the CEO review process. The audit committee, already familiar with the company's information system, is an ideal group to monitor and improve the information directors are receiving. The nominating committee, in addition to evaluating individual directors, can orchestrate the annual review of the board's activities by the full board. Each committee thus makes a unique contribution to the board's oversight of its own functioning.

In the past decade, employee empowerment has improved productivity and quality, allowing many U.S. companies to be more competitive in the global marketplace. Empowering directors will enable them and their organizations to deal more successfully with the turbulence and demands of the future. U.S. companies today face more challenges and uncertainty than at any time since the end of World War II. The continuing growth of the world's marketplace, with customers and competition in Asia, Eastern Europe, and South America, as well as the shift in the domestic economy caused by the decline in defense spending and changes in the health care system, among other factors, present U.S. companies with unprecedented challenges and opportunities. Empowered boards are most likely to contribute to meeting them if their growing power is developed in collaboration with that of the managers they oversee. That means both groups must work together to establish and understand the role of empowered directors.

Originally published in January–February 1995
Reprint 95107

A New Tool for Boards

The Strategic Audit

GORDON DONALDSON

Executive Summary

WITH INSTITUTIONAL INVESTORS, regulatory authorities, the financial press, and the fear of lawsuits all pressuring boards of public corporations to be more active, many directors are seeking practical ways to conduct strategic oversight. Gordon Donaldson's strategic audit provides an orderly way for boards to review strategy without invading management's territory.

Usually, there are three triggers that motivate boards to get involved in strategy: the retirement of a CEO, a precipitous decline in profitability, or an unsolicited takeover attempt. These triggers force a board into a reactive mode and are not conducive to effective oversight. A case in point is the attempted takeover of CPC International in 1986, which forced the board and the CEO to admit that their hopes for the corn wet-milling business had not been based on a realistic assessment of past performance. Had a strategic audit been in place, they might have spotted trouble in a timely fashion.

Managers are expected to turn strategic vision into operational reality, but directors represent shareholders and must evaluate strategy based on how the company's returns compare with those of other investment opportunities. Donaldson suggest that a low-key, behind-the-scenes audit of strategy, designed to lend credibility to management's leadership and not undermine it, is an important board tool.

A strategic audit committee should be made up of outside directors who meet every three years to evaluate strategy using objective financial measurements with which both the directors and the CEO are thoroughly comfortable. Effective strategic oversight can anticipate problems and show shareholders that boards and CEOs have a joint commitment to effective and orderly governance.

In THE AFTERMATH of the wave of restructuring that peaked in the 1980s, the corporate oversight process has received unprecedented public attention, and investor activism has resulted in numerous proposals for reform. Board members, seeing the number of stockholder lawsuits and the escalating cost of directors' and officers' liability insurance, are feeling pressure from their increased risk as well. Even more important is the pressure from holders of large blocks of stock (pension and mutual funds), from judicial and regulatory authorities, and from the financial press— all of whom are calling for boards to be more active.

This attention has had an impact on the nation's public corporations and has brought about a change in boardroom behavior that is significant, if often imperceptible to outsiders. Outside board members are now much more willing to stake out independent positions in boardroom discussions and, at times, even openly oppose the chief executive when they believe the vital interests of the corporation are at stake. Recently, directors' independence led to the ouster of the incumbent chairman or the CEO at Morrison Knudsen, W.R. Grace, and KMart.

Efforts to reform the governance process have also intensified. Investors and investors' advocates, impatient with the sporadic nature and rate of change, have proposed legal, regulatory, and structural improvements in the relationships among shareholders, boards of directors, and CEOs. Some proposals call for radical changes in the rules governing the election of directors at public corporations. Some recommend adopting certain attributes of the private corporation. Indeed, Michael C. Jensen ("Eclipse of the Public Corporation," HBR September–October 1989) predicted that in such industries as banking and food processing the public corporation will decline, to be replaced by new forms of organization, such as the LBO partnership. Other proposals are designed to address specific issues, such as directors' compensation or the separation of the offices of board chair and CEO.

One problem I see with many of the reform initiatives is that they are concerned only with the broad principles of governance and offer little practical guidance. More important, these proposals do not directly address the fundamental issue at the heart of investors' concern— namely, the capacity of the board to intervene in the face of an unsuccessful or ailing business strategy. Proposals to strengthen that ability are among the most important to consider but are also the most difficult to gain consensus on and to implement.

Board Oversight and Company Strategy

Board involvement in formulating and implementing corporate strategy has always been a sensitive issue. Although it is standard procedure for managers to brief directors on the evolving strategy and structure at the annual meeting dedicated to that purpose, it has always been understood that the "ownership" of the current strategy remains firmly in the hands of the chief executive and his or her management team. And for good reason. In order to be effective, every organization requires not only a clear and unambiguous strategic mission but also the confidence that its top management has the authority and ability to carry it out. By nature, the typical board of directors is poorly designed and ill equipped to provide hands-on product and market leadership. The majority of its members usually lack the industry-specific experience, the company-specific knowledge, and, most important, the time necessary to turn broad strategic vision into operational reality. Board members give their undivided attention at most once a month for six or eight hours at a time. They can hardly be expected to have the detailed command of the issues and the requisite independent judgment necessary to make compelling proposals to counter those of management.

In addition, the typical board meeting is an inappropriate forum for raising serious concerns about a company's strategic direction. All who have served as board members know that attending a board meeting is rather like entering the on-ramp of an expressway at rush hour: You spend half the time getting up to speed and the other half trying to insert yourself into the bumper-to-bumper boardroom traffic, only to find that it is time to exit and try again a month later. The customary agenda is set by the chair and invariably focuses on details of implementing the ongoing business strategy. Presentations reflect the urgent pursuit of the company's established mission, and managers are likely to be impatient with board members who do not share their total commitment to the chosen path. Therefore, the regular board meeting is an unsuitable, even hostile, environment for revealing serious reservations about the underlying strategic assumptions.

Of course, individual board members, such as the company's founder, a major investor, or a former CEO, have often exerted considerable influence over strategic direction, although usually behind the scenes. Absent such unique personal prerogatives, board members are expected to serve as supportive critics of the strategy in place. Those who choose to violate the norms of boardroom debate by aggressively and persistently challenging corporate leadership—thereby invading the DMZ between board and executive—run the risk of finding themselves isolated and, in time, replaced. Without an established forum for vigorous debate, serious concerns either simmer in one-on-one discussions outside the boardroom or boil over in messy and destructive confrontations in front of subordinate managers, who are invariably present at board meetings. Both outcomes are unacceptable. As a result, outside board members seeking a change in strategy or, perhaps, leadership are wary, and examples of spontaneous intervention are relatively few and far between.

If these interventions occur at all, they seem to do so under one of three circumstances, as I describe in my book *Corporate Restructuring: Managing the Change Process from Within* (Harvard Business School Press, 1994). The most common is the retirement of the incumbent chief executive, even though the retiring CEO frequently nominates his or her successor. A second circumstance is a sudden, precipitous decline in profitability or asset value, as in the case of Morrison Knudsen. A third occasion that might trigger intervention is an external challenge threatening a change in control—the classic barbarian at the gates. Such a scenario was common in the 1980s, the heyday of corporate raiders, and so weakened incumbent chief executives that there was often an opportunity for boards to seize the initiative.

But the threat of one or all of these events is insufficient to guarantee vigilant oversight. A strategy may go sour long before the normal retirement date of the CEO responsible for choosing it. Evidence that a strategy is failing is more commonly seen in gradual or erratic erosion of profitability than in dramatic collapse.

Boards can fulfill strategic oversight duties better if they implement a formal review process: a strategic audit.

The barbarian may be off on other quests and may never show up at the gates, or, if he does, may be persuaded to go away. The worst characteristic of the three triggers is that the transforming event comes from outside the governance process and forces both management and board into a reactive mode.

Even when decisive intervention is initiated from within the governance process, it is usually not initiated by a formal action of the full board. What happens instead is that one board member impulsively steps forward to assume leadership and to provoke other independent members into unified action. Probably the best known example is John Smale's 1992 move on behalf of the GM board to replace chairman and CEO Robert Stempel. Like the three triggers I describe, such an approach is an unreliable mechanism of board oversight and seems unnecessarily disruptive.

Therefore, the question remains: Is it possible to create a formal mechanism within the existing governance process so that the board can exercise proactively its responsibility for strategic oversight? My answer is yes. The mechanism is a formal strategic-review process—a strategic audit—which imposes its own discipline on both the board and management, much as the financial audit process does. I believe such an audit can be designed to stand the test of time and survive the inevitable disputes over authority. The process would center the leadership of strategic oversight in the hands of independent directors and provide them with the authority to establish both the criteria for and the methods of review. It would further require the board and the CEO to hold a regular, joint review of company performance. And it would signal to the investing public that both the board and management accept the board's authority and responsibility for active, ongoing strategic oversight.

THE CASE OF CPC INTERNATIONAL

In the summer of 1986, financial analysts began to speculate that CPC International, a leading manufacturer of food products in the United States and abroad, was ripe for major restructuring. In the early fall, the tone and content of the speculation changed as investor discontent grew, and word on the street was that CPC was being considered for a takeover by ConAgra, Revlon, or an inside management group. These rumors turned into reality in October, when an investment group headed by Ronald O. Perelman attempted an unsolicited takeover. Could this outside intervention have been avoided? Quite possibly, if the board had had a formal strategic-review process in place. It is just such an event that a strategic audit is designed to avoid. It is helpful to review the events in the CPC case leading up to the Perelman raid to see how a review process might have worked.

Corn Products was founded in 1906 with the development of a wet-milling process to refine corn by-products—corn starch, syrup, and oil—for both consumer and industrial use. In 1958, it merged with Best Foods, which was a grocery products company with well-known brands. At the time of the merger, however, the company was dominated by the wet-milling division, which was in a capital-intensive, high-volume, low-margin industry subject to periodic bouts of competitive overbuilding. The intent of combining the two businesses—later renamed CPC International—was to diversify the product line and enhance opportunities for growth and profitability in consumer products.

Beginning around 1980, the profitability of corn refining underwent serious, steady erosion because of overcapacity in the industry, and a widening gap developed between the performance of the corn by-products and that of consumer foods. For example, in 1977, the return on assets (ROA) in consumer products was 24.4% and in corn refining, 12.6%; but by 1983, the ROA in consumer foods was 25.5% and in corn refining, only 6.6%.

Despite these data, management remained committed to its traditional revenue base in corn refining and to a long-term strategy based on the expectation of improving competitive performance in that industry. And management made no attempt to conceal from shareholders the effect its strategy was having on performance. Indeed, over an 18-year period beginning in 1974, CPC consistently used its annual report to present comparative data on the components of its corporate return on equity. Furthermore, the data were presented for the current year and the four preceding years in an identical format each time. It is rare for a public corporation to maintain such consistency and even more unusual for it to keep reporting the drivers of equity value over such a turbulent period in its history.

Although the actual disparity in performance between corn refining and consumer products was difficult to observe early on, it was impossible to conceal during the period from 1983 to 1985, when there was a short-term decline in the profitability of the consumer foods line. As the data reveal, CPC reported a dramatic decline in the corporate return on equity from 18.5% to 10.5%, turning a public spotlight on the milling operations' persistent drag on earnings. (See the exhibit "The Strategic Audit Report Card for CPC 1977-1989.") Capital market analysts and the financial press began to suggest that CPC should divest all or part of the milling business and release the full market value of the Best Foods product line to investors.

There is no record of what went on in the CPC boardroom at the time of this unfavorable public attention. We do not know whether any of the board members challenged the wisdom of the strategy in place, although

The Strategic Audit Report Card for CPC 1977–1989

If a strategic audit process had been in place before 1985, CPC's board might have preempted the 1986 takeover attempt.

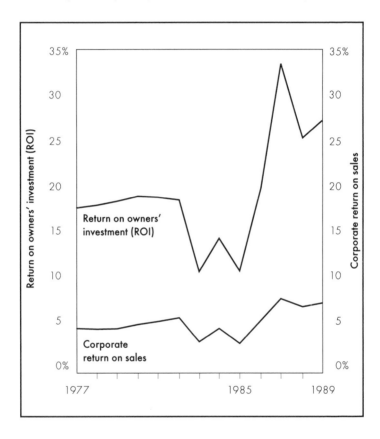

Through 1985, lower margins in corn wet-milling contributed to a declining corporate profit margin. Reduced leverage and the declining turnover of assets exaggerated the erosion in return on owners' investment (ROI). After 1985, and subsequent to restructuring, corporate margins improved, largely because of the increased emphasis on higher-margin, branded consumer products. CPC saw a dramatic and immediate gain in ROI in 1987, with continued improvement in asset turnover and use of leverage.

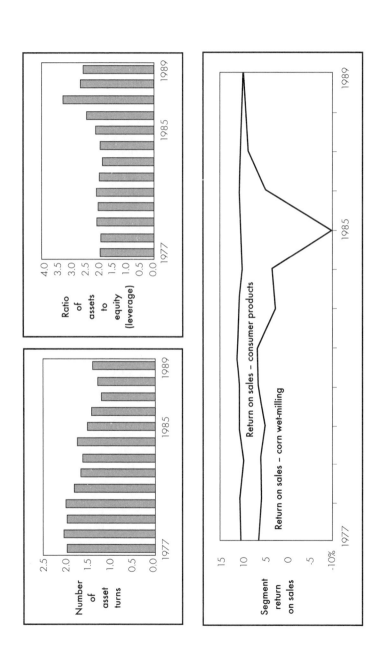

the speed of management's response to subsequent events suggests that either the board or management—or both—had previously analyzed and debated alternatives to the strategy. Certainly the board could not plead that it lacked objective historical evidence on the inherent weaknesses of the business. The takeover attempt by Perelman occurred two years into the tenure of new CEO James Eiszner and forced his hand. He mounted a vigorous and successful defense, implementing many of the changes advocated by outside critics, including the divestiture of CPC's substantial corn wet-milling division in Europe.

If CPC had had a strategic review process in place before the downturn, past performance would have signaled trouble.

The outcome of the restructuring was immediately apparent in CPC's financial performance in 1987 and was reflected in rising market values for CPC stock as well. However, the costs of restructuring under the guns of a battle for control were substantial. In addition to the legal costs, there were the costs of negotiations conducted in haste and from a position of weakness—namely, the sale of underpriced assets and the repurchase of overpriced stock. And there was a management team preoccupied with staying in office rather than doing the job it was hired to do.

So CPC's turnaround was dramatic and positive, but the costs of lost time and opportunities were high. This much we know. I suggest we can also be sure of another thing. If a formal board-level strategic-review process had been well established before the downturn between 1983 and 1985, periodic discussions about strategic direction between the board and management would have centered not on optimistic promises for the future but on the pessimistic realities of past performance. Set against the backdrop of public debate and investor discontent over the strategy, these discussions could well have resulted in a less costly and painful readjustment of the company's strategic path.

The Board's Unique Perspective

There will be some who resist the idea of another strategic-review process on top of management's existing annual reviews and reports. They will say, Isn't this overkill? Shouldn't review be a joint effort with management? Isn't management best qualified to select the appropriate criteria to evaluate the company's progress within its industry?

The answer to all these questions is no. Management and the board have unique and distinct perspectives on strategy. Managers are charged with turning strategic vision into operational reality. Of necessity, they must focus on one strategic path at a time and pursue it relentlessly to maximize its potential for corporate profitability. If managers equivocate, they default on their obligations to employees and shareholders alike, eroding much-needed morale and commitment. In this context, the best standard of performance by which to motivate the organization is a relative one—to ask how the company is performing relative to previous strategies, relative to the results of last quarter or last year, relative to the best competitors in the same product markets. But performance evaluation designed to motivate the people in an organization is not intended to challenge the chosen path.

The board's mandate in strategic oversight is distinctly different. Its responsibility is to represent the perspective of investors and question the strategic path itself. The board's evaluation of the validity of the existing strategy mustn't be based simply on the performance of the company relative to itself, its industry, or its past performance, but rather on comparisons between returns derived from the current strategy and those possible from other strategies. Management may think it's dealing with disloyal boards at times, but from directors' perspective, they are the "loyal opposition."

Although the two perspectives converge when board and managers are *developing* strategy, management's role in *executing* the strategy precludes it from also objectively evaluating the strategic path once it is in place. The strategic audit, therefore, must be directed by independent board members rather than by management insiders. And the board—not management—should select the key criteria to monitor strategic results.

Elements of the Strategic Audit

ESTABLISHING THE CRITERIA

The most important requirement for the data used in the strategic review process is that they be objective. In addition, the criteria should be familiar, well-understood, and accepted measures of financial performance. There are two reasons why. First, the ultimate responsibility of the board is to understand the impact of a given strategy on the value of the owners' investment. This obligation implies evaluating performance in financial terms. Second, although it's inevitable that much of the evidence on the success of an evolving strategy is subjective, managers' familiarity with the details of product-market and company-specific issues, and their access to an incredible amount and variety of data give them an advantage over outside board members. Objective data consistently presented and reinforced by the cumulative evidence of past performance can strengthen the power and credibility of the board's opinion. Standard financial indicators facilitate discussion in terms all parties can understand.

Some will argue that using such indicators is just one more example of a myopic preoccupation with the corporate bottom line, leading to short-term decisions that erode long-term competitive strength and profitability in domestic and international product markets. I must disagree.

Standard financial indicators facilitate discussion in terms all parties can understand.

Although I think that financial criteria should be the central focus of board oversight, I do not think such a focus prevents the board from considering other kinds of progress. It should certainly weigh all objective—or even subjective—evidence of strategic progress demonstrating long-term competitive superiority. But it is equally important for the board to intervene when it sees persistent, long-term erosion of the investment base, on which all corporate activity depends.

The criteria best suited to the strategic oversight process share two important characteristics. They focus on the sustainable rate of return on shareholder investment produced by the corporate income stream. They also permit objective comparisons among the company's separable income streams and with alternative investments in other companies inside or outside the industry. These data should help the board determine whether the company's chosen strategy—or a particular decision—will contribute to a long-term return of shareholder investment equal or superior to other investment alternatives of comparable risk. They should also allow a comparison of the promise of future returns with the reality of past performance.

In the final analysis, these criteria should reflect a fundamental economic reality: The long-term loyalty of the equity holders depends solely on sustaining a competitive return on investment. Without that, no product-market strategy is safe. Although professional managers might find this dictum hard to accept, it is nevertheless the reality of the public capital markets in which they operate. Just doing better than other immediate investment alternatives, better than last year, or even better than all major competitors in the same industry may not, in the end, be good enough to justify continued investor support.

With this in mind, boards will find that several criteria satisfy the basic requirements of a strategic review process. One is the reported return on book investment (ROI), particularly when it is disaggregated into its primary components, as shown in the exhibit. It has the advantage of being based on data familiar to shareholders and management. It shows profit per unit of sales (profit margin), sales per unit of capital employed (asset turnover), and capital employed per unit of equity invested (leverage). When multiplied together, these ratios transform profit margin into return on equity.

This particular set of measurements has two weaknesses, however. First, it may be subject to random changes in accounting practice, so that users may have to make appropriate retroactive adjustments to the raw data. In addition, it doesn't provide an external standard of comparison. The underlying components of the corporate income stream need to be broken out, and comparable data on companies inside and outside the industry gathered. The data of review should also encompass information on investor response, including price-to-earnings and market-to-book-value ratios. These data reveal evidence of investors' reaction to published information on company performance and are a measure of confidence. They are an essential supplement to any measurement based primarily on company-specific data.

Other commonly used criteria for the evaluation of strategic alternatives are:

- *Cash flow return on investment (CFROI).* This measure highlights net cash flows from operations rather than reported income and produces a rate of return that can be compared with alternative company or market rates of return (the cost of capital). It has the special merit of approximating actual flows of investable funds and is therefore well suited to rate-of-return comparisons with alternative investment opportunities.

- *Net economic value added from year to year (EVA).* This is an estimate of the absolute dollar value that is added to shareholder wealth whenever a company gains a return on investment in excess of its cost of capital. EVA incorporates the same basic variables of CFROI but expresses the evidence in a dramatic way. It highlights those periods in which, in comparison with alternative investment opportunities, the company's performance has led to the creation—or destruction—of economic value.

- *Total of shareholders' return on investment (TSR).* This measures the actual year-to-year taxable income received by shareholders in the form of dividends plus capital gains as a percentage of beginning-of-year market value. Unlike the other three measures mentioned, TSR has the advantage of reflecting value in hand rather than value in prospect. It is more a measure of stockholders' expectations than of demonstrated return on corporate capital employed, and it has the disadvantage of reflecting short-term and often exaggerated fluctuations of the stock market as a whole, for which management cannot be held responsible. For this reason, TSR is probably best used as a supplement to one of the other three measures mentioned.

Each of the measures I describe has its strengths and weaknesses, but one simple consideration should drive the choice of the particular measure—or set of measures—for a given company: The directors and the chief executive alike must have a thorough grasp of all the elements of the chosen measurement. Otherwise, debate over the validity of the index itself may undermine the impact of the objective evidence. If particular members of the board are more familiar with other indices, there might not be universal agreement about which to use for the audit. In such a case, individual members might be provided with the comparable data in the index of their choice. What all the measures I have presented share is an ability to capture significant and sustained trends, whether strong or weak, which then become the baseline from which to track strategic progress.

The board must not only choose the measures and control the database but also remain alert to varied signs of weakness.

DATABASE DESIGN AND MAINTENANCE

An effective strategic-oversight process requires that the board take control not only of the criteria of performance but also of the database in which the criteria are maintained. One of the problems that outside board members often have in evaluating strategic performance is that all the information they receive passes through the filter of a management perspective. In addition, data often come with limited historical reference and in a format that does not map to the previous one. Insiders may consider the presentation meaningful, or at least well intentioned; but outsiders may feel confused and end up misinformed. The credibility of the board's review process depends on the integrity and consistency of the statistics by which progress is measured. Typically, it will be the cumulative evidence that tracks emerging trends in the indices of performance over several quarters or years.

Effective oversight depends on how these data are assembled and maintained in the short and long term and who does the job on behalf of the board. Traditionally, boards of directors have neither the independent staff support nor the personal time and expertise to devote to data collection and analysis. One solution is to ask the company's chief financial officer for the help of someone on staff. This solution has some obvious practical problems, however. Conflict of interest could arise for an employee working with potentially sensitive data. Certainly issues of divided loyalties will come up if the employee uncovers data that could cause a problem for an in-house boss or for the company. And to the outside observer, a company employee acting as the "independent" liaison to the board is a contradiction in terms.

A better solution is for an outside consultant to design the database and gather the data the board chooses to monitor. The database maintenance function could become an ongoing contractual arrangement. The management challenge here would be to provide a consultant from the outside with enough information and context about the company that he or she could ask intelligent questions about the database design and data collection effort. At least initially, the board and its consultant would need a great deal of cooperation and assistance from management. The board would also need to be very familiar with details of the database design and reporting activities in order to ensure continuity if the consulting arrangement changes over time.

My preferred solution, one consistent with the model of the financial audit, is to involve the company's public auditors. Their assignment could be like that of an outside consultant in design and data collection, but the public auditors would bring much more to the ongoing effort because of their access to and familiarity with the company's financial information and systems. Their role would ensure, over the long term, consistency in maintenance, documentation, and reporting. Management would not have to be involved in establishing the relationship or in acting as a go-between.

THE STRATEGIC AUDIT COMMITTEE

As we have already established, there is no existing mechanism in most governance processes for formal strategic oversight. A sustainable, effective process means assigning specific responsibility and leadership to particular members of the board, in much the same way that other committee assignments are made. The strategic audit committee's charter is not complicated, but it should cover the issues I have addressed. The committee should select the criteria for review of strategic performance, oversee the design of the database, and establish a review process. It should ensure the integrity and continuity of the ongoing data collection and reporting efforts, identify issues for discussion with the CEO, keep the full board abreast of the evidence, and schedule both regular and special meetings.

I suggest that the outside directors select three of their own members to form the committee. The selection of the chair is particularly important. If the board has an outside director who is the lead or liaison, he or she would be a natural choice to chair the strategic audit committee as well. In the event of a difference of opinion over strategy between the chief executive and outside board members, having the liaison director chair the committee will reduce the possibility that the leadership of the outside board members will be divided. As with the financial audit committee, committee membership should rotate on a staggered basis to preserve institutional memory. All outside directors should have a turn on the strategic audit committee before their time on the board is up.

The frequency of meetings will depend on the nature of the industry and the rapidity of change in the technological, competitive, and social environment. In addition to periodic presentations to the full board and absent a special need, such as the impending retirement of the chief executive, I suggest that the committee meet once every three years. Meetings should not be so frequent that strategic review is confused with an operating review or that the minor changes in key indicators are incorrectly interpreted as significant trends. Moreover, the board's normal oversight process must not imply that the CEO is on a short leash or that the leadership is constantly up for grabs.

RELATIONSHIPS WITH THE CEO

A central objective of a well-designed and -implemented strategic-oversight process is to reduce both the appearance and the reality of confrontation over disputed turf. The robust egos that normally inhabit the boardroom are highly sensitive to actions that appear to challenge their authority. Even though potential overlap between responsibility and oversight occurs throughout the entire management structure, it is a particularly delicate issue at this level. Every time the question of "the right strategic direction" comes up spontaneously and unexpectedly, there is a risk that it will be perceived as implicit criticism of the strategy in place and of the leadership. It takes sensitivity and diplomacy to raise such issues constructively, but sensitivity and diplomacy are attributes not all board members possess.

Normally, the committee would be a low-key operation that would add to management's credibility.

On the other hand, a regular, formal review process dedicated to the discussion of strategic performance with the CEO reduces the likelihood of an adversarial atmosphere. Equally important to a calm and thoughtful exchange of views are meetings in which the only people present are the outside board members and the chief executive. Differences of opinion can be kept private until they are amicably resolved or, if they can't be kept private, their public consequences can be thoroughly considered. The strategic audit committee is not meant to share in the leadership of the ongoing business strategy or be a backseat driver. Under normal circumstances, it should be a low-key, behind-the-scenes operation designed to lend additional credibility to management's leadership and authority.

ALERTNESS TO DUTY

Even with the imposed discipline of a well-designed, formal oversight process, a board can fall asleep at the controls. A period of sustained success can lull the board into the belief that success is forever and that the company can do very nicely on automatic pilot. It is essential that the board be alert both to signs of weakness in the established strategic mission and to events or initiatives that present a natural opportunity to confirm or modify the existing strategic direction.

The board must understand that every time it gives its approval to an investment proposal that enlarges the scope or extends the term of an existing business strategy, it is openly signaling to the entire management team that it supports that strategy. Because investment or funding proposals, large and small, come in a steady stream, the board cannot be constantly attaching reservations or qualifications to its approval. Such concerns should be reserved for the periodic review meetings between the outside board members and the CEO— meetings triggered by the strategic audit committee.

Nevertheless, some events may justify a special meeting of the strategic audit committee. In 1983, the board of CPC was no doubt well aware of the persistently poor performance of corn wet-milling and of its drag on equity values and corporate return on equity. But despite the facts of past performance, management was persistently optimistic about long-term improvement. For those board members who were disposed to cut back or terminate corn wet-milling, the downturn in the consumer foods business and the highly visible decline in corporate return on equity would have been a golden opportunity to bring the issue to a head. Another opportunity for strategic review came with the initiation in 1984 of a new $1.5 billion "Investment for Growth" program, which was primarily for corn wet-milling facilities. Unfortunately, these openings for board intervention were preempted by Ronald Perelman's takeover attempt.

Alertness to duty and to opportunity is the capstone of a serious strategic-review process. CPC's board passed up good opportunities. Such natural turning points are often occasions when management and the organization are best prepared—and even eager—to consider strategic redirection.

BY FOCUSING AS HEAVILY as I do on measurements and data relating to the creation of corporate and shareholder wealth, I appear to neglect the governance obligation to gather data on other organizational and social consequences of strategic choice. For example, although both growth and diversification may at times erode equity value, these objectives have traditionally been the means of attracting and retaining the best professional and management talent. Both were common corporate priorities in the 1970s but came under increasing criticism from the investment community in the 1980s. The significant restructuring that followed was directed at downsizing the corporate overhead acquired in years of high profit and accelerated growth, shedding peripheral activities with low profitability and marginal corporate synergy, and refocusing on core competence and long-term competitive advantage.

Every successful business activity involves the effective cooperation of several distinct constituencies— employees, unions, suppliers, customers, host communities, and shareholders—and they all have legitimate needs. Board oversight requires a broad perspective, and any strategic consequence that affects the ability of the organization to reach and sustain its full, long-term competitive potential will demand board attention. However, in the end, a given strategy must deliver a competitive return on shareholder investment.

Of course, no organizational process can guarantee that the people involved will do everything that with 20/20 hindsight seems obvious. On the other hand, a process ensuring that independent board members and the chief executive meet in private and focus on objective evidence about the strategy in place is the best guarantee that well-informed, orderly, and timely strategic change will spring from the established governance process.

Pursued in a spirit of mutual respect, the process facilitates ongoing, constructive dialogue.

Some chief executives will see a potential for mischief in the formation of a formal strategic-audit process plus a further burden on their already overburdened schedule. However, the pressures for more vigorous oversight by corporate boards are now well established, and the likely alternative responses—new legal or regulatory intervention or more frequent random outbursts of boardroom vigilance—cannot be preferable.

The process I suggest, if implemented in a spirit of mutual respect, opens opportunities for a sincere, ongoing, private dialogue about the strategic mission—a dialogue based on objective evidence, free of the imposed deadlines and undesirable distractions of sudden events and external intervention. It increases the possibility that a shared understanding will lead to evolutionary change in strategic direction, serving the best interests of all concerned. Chief executives and boards of directors need a formal and visible review process to demonstrate to shareholders their shared commitment to orderly and effective governance.

Originally published in July–August 1995
Reprint 95404

The Promise of the Governed Corporation

JOHN POUND

Executive Summary

AT ITS CORE, corporate governance is not about power but about ensuring that decisions are made effectively. That is why reforms of power relationships will not by themselves create more smoothly run organizations. What is needed is a system in which senior managers and the board truly collaborate on decisions and both regularly seek the input of shareholders.

In most companies, the role of the governance system is only to put the right managers in place, monitor their progress, and replace them when they fail. Neither the board nor shareholders offer opinions on strategy or policy unless managers are clearly failing. The problem with such a model is that most corporate failures result from a few flawed decisions rather than outright incompetence. That model plays into the weaknesses of human behavior by allowing mistakes to go uncorrected until they become catastrophes.

The first step to improving a company's governance system is rethinking the role of directors. They must have expertise in the company's industry and in finance; meeting procedures should focus on new strategies, not just on reviewing past performance; directors need better access to company information; they should be required to devote substantial time to the corporation; and their compensations should be linked to stock performance. Second, managers, board members, and shareholders must set up lines of regular and direct communication.

A number of companies have already made progress toward governance that focuses less on the competence of the CEO and more on the effectiveness of the organization, but change will come slowly. The promise of a well-governed corporation is more new ideas, more adaptable decision making, and better accountability to markets.

THE DEBATE OVER CORPORATE GOVERNANCE has long centered on power. The goal has been to tighten control over wayward managers. Recent reform initiatives have included conducting more formal audits of management performance, separating the positions of chief executive officer and chair, appointing lead outside directors, and making a company's board members more accountable to its outside shareholders.

But reforms that shift power from one party to another will not by themselves create more smoothly run, profitable organizations. The reason? They do not address the fundamental problems in corporate governance, which stem not from power imbalances but from failures in the corporate decision-making process.

The focus on power is driven by a model of governance I call the *managed corporation*. In that model, senior managers are responsible for leadership and decision making. The board's function is to hire top-level managers, monitor them, and fire them if they do not perform. Shareholders' only role is to throw out the board if the corporation does not perform. Indeed, shareholders are generally treated as if they cannot assess corporate policy for themselves but must depend on managers and directors to do so for them.

The managed-corporation model, a legacy of the rise of large public companies and dispersed shareholders, has dominated the corporate arena for decades. But in today's business environment, it does not make sense.

Corporate governance is not, at its core, about power; it is about finding ways to ensure that decisions are made effectively.

Most managers do not have excess power, and most corporate failures are not the result of power imbalances. Instead, failures usually result from a few well-intentioned but flawed management decisions that are not challenged in an efficient, effective manner. Corporate failures occur because of subtle failures in the decision-making process—in how boards and managers make decisions and monitor corporate progress.

Power-based reforms are not the key to correcting the problem. To be sure, the balance of power is important. But, at its core, corporate governance is not about power; it is about ensuring effective decision making. Corporate governance reform should seek ways to create and maintain an efficient decision-making process. The goal should be to prevent significant mistakes in corporate strategy and to ensure that the mistakes that do occur can be corrected quickly.

Ultimately, what is needed is a system in which senior managers and the board truly collaborate on decision making. In addition, both directors and managers should actively seek the input of institutional shareholders. Institutions are no longer the passive constituents of the managed-corporation model; they have emerged as serious players in the governance process.

The new model can be called the *governed corporation* because it reconnects two critical parts of the corporate governance equation—shareholders and board members—to the decision-making process. Reforms based on the governed-corporation model do not revolve around power shifts. Instead, they center on roles and behavior. (See the exhibit "The Managed Corporation Versus the Governed Corporation.") The result is a positive change in the way companies debate, review, and decide policy.

The Managed Corporation and Corporate Failure

To get beyond the philosophy of governance created by the managed corporation, directors, shareholders, and senior managers must first understand that philosophy and the problems it causes.

The basic premises of the managed-corporation model can be found in any modern writing on corporate strategy or governance. Its rise early in the twentieth century reflected both the dispersion of corporate ownership among many shareholders and the emergence of a new class of professional managers who were neither large stockholders nor founders of corporations. Dispersed ownership meant that shareholders were no longer involved in setting corporate policy. There was thus a need for leadership. Senior managers were the answer: they shaped the corporation in an era of

---

The Managed Corporation Versus the Governed Corporation: Boardroom Paradigms and Practices

The Managed-Corporation Paradigm	The Governed-Corporation Paradigm
The board's role is to hire, monitor, and, when necessary, replace management.	*The board's role is to foster effective decisions and reverse failed policies.*
Board Characteristics	**Board Characteristics**
Power sufficient to control the CEO and the evaluation process	Expertise sufficient to allow the board to add value to the decision-making process
Independence to ensure that the CEO is honestly evaluated and that directors are not compromised by conflicts or co-opted by management	Incentives to ensure that the board is committed to creating corporate value
Board procedures that allow outside directors to evaluate managers dispassionately and effectively	Procedures that foster open debate and keep board members informed and attuned to the shareholders' concerns
Policies	**Policies**
Separate the CEO and chair (or lead outside director)	Required areas of expertise that must be represented on the board, such as core industry and finance
Board meetings without CEO present	Minimum time commitment of 25 days
Committee of independent directors to evaluate the CEO	Large option packages for directors
Independent financial and legal advisors to outside directors	Designated critic to question new policy proposals
Explicit yardsticks for judging the CEO's performance	Regular meetings with large shareholders
	Board members free to request information from any employee

absentee owners. In the model of the managed corporation, therefore, managers led, and directors and shareholders followed. The role of the governance system was to put the right managers in place, monitor their progress, and replace them when they failed—a paradigm that has carried through to this day.

In the managed corporation, shareholders and boards are held distant from strategy formulation and policy setting. A major business question might be debated at the board level, but the assumption is that unless the managers are irrational or dishonest, or have a terrible long-term performance record, they should be given the room to implement their chosen strategy. Board members are expected to challenge policies only if there is evidence of performance failure. Otherwise, if directors are troubled by a company's strategies, the message is that they should get off the board or find themselves another CEO.

The managed corporation also discourages board members and managers from taking into account, let alone taking seriously, the opinions of outside shareholders. Shareholders are supposed to protect their interests by replacing boards that perform poorly. As a consequence, when shareholders seek to exert influence over policy, board members and managers often do not listen. If shareholders persist and their concerns appear to be widespread, managers and board members feel threatened. Indeed, the louder shareholders' voices, the more likely managers and board members will shut them out in fear of a challenge for control.

If the major cause of corporate failure were management incompetence, the governance system fostered by the managed-corporation model would work. But most performance crises are the result of errors that arise not from incompetence but from failures of judgment. As a result, the model fosters an unstable cycle of silence and crisis.

Errors arise from the simple realities of human decision making and organizational behavior. People make mistakes. Individuals tend to be biased toward decisions and strategies that favor their own personal strengths. People also have a difficult time confronting past failures, as the well-known psychological phenomenon of cognitive dissonance explains. In fact, research in psychology documents that both individuals and groups become more firmly committed to past decisions, the worse the evidence becomes on how the decision is working out in practice. Managers who stick with failed policies in the face of dismal performance, and directors who stick with failed policies in the face of shareholder discomfort, are both displaying a well-documented pathology of judgment and behavior.

Add to that the natural reluctance of individuals to challenge the status quo. In hierarchical organizations, junior managers often do not feel comfortable challenging decisions because doing so might stymie their advancement. As information travels upward, bad news is filtered out. Within the corporation, then, the job of challenge falls to the CEO's peers

Differentiating between good and bad decisions may mean delving into company politics.

and advisers—the directors. But board members also tend to be biased in favor of collegiality and consensus. For one, it is easier than provoking a conflict. For another, although they may suspect that a particular decision is wrong, directors in most cases have little evidence on which to base a debate. In large organizations, most board members are not on site and have little direct, personal contact with product markets. Without evidence, they are reluctant to speak up. Board members who challenge a policy risk being wrong and damaging their reputations. Those behavioral realities also explain why the corporate governance reforms suggested by economists, such as takeovers and leveraged buyouts, do not work over the long term. (See "The Limits of Economic Solutions" at the end of this article.)

The reticence is further exacerbated by the political complexity of decision making at the top levels of a corporation. Personalities intrude. Points of view differ. For the board member, trying to differentiate between good and bad decisions may mean delving into organizational politics and probing personal agendas. That can be awkward and uncomfortable. What's more, the individuals under scrutiny may discourage such attention.

Every now and then, a case bubbles over into the public eye that casts the political realities of organizations into sharp relief. In 1994, John P. Reilly, president of Brunswick Corporation, a maker of boats and other recreational products, resigned despite rebounding corporate performance. Reilly had been on the job nine months and was considered heir apparent to chairman and CEO Jack F. Reichert, but he reportedly had clashes with a senior vice president. In a *Wall Street Journal* article, the company attributed his departure to "philosophical and cultural differences," while Reilly was reported to have called the corporation "dysfunctional." The precise locus of blame is irrelevant. What matters is that the politics of the organization provoked the departure.

Finally, one must take into account the corporate life cycle. Many corporate failures occur because the team of decision makers is tired. Managers get set in their ways.

The founders who were once innovators run out of ideas. If dialogue is discouraged, who reenergizes the corporate organization and how? What forces catalyze a new era of entrepreneurship?

The managed-corporation model plays into the weaknesses of human and organizational behavior and allows mistakes to go uncorrected until they become catastrophes. It also does not encourage corporate renewal. Consider the chain of events at one small Midwestern tool manufacturer with $50 million in sales. The company had built a franchise in a line of high-end products sold through hardware stores. In the late 1970s, the retail market began to change. There were increasing numbers of large discount retailers, which were less interested in carrying complex, high-end products. In response, the CEO decided to enter the retail market directly, opening small company-owned stores across the country. But the management team had no retail skills, and the operations were troubled. Retail expansion continued for ten years despite losses. Profits in manufacturing kept the company alive and funded the retail disaster. Then, in the early 1990s, the recession hit and the company went into crisis.

Throughout the 1980s, the company's board allowed the flawed retail strategy to proceed despite clear evidence that managers lacked retail skills and that the expansion was becoming a black hole. The board's reticence continued even as a sliding stock price caused some investors to express concern and others to desert the company. Some members of the board later acknowledged that it had been a mistake to allow management to continue to pursue its retail objectives. But they had not intervened, because they had followed the protocols suggested by the managed corporation. They had regu-

larly assessed the company's overall performance but
had never felt they could question the management
team's competence. In a troubled industry, continuing
profits in manufacturing had kept the company above
water. Because the senior managers were not clearly failing, the board let them pursue their chosen strategy. Of
course, in retrospect, the board's intervention to reverse
the failed retail strategy could have saved the company.

Another example is the case of Picadilly Cafeterias.
Picadilly, a chain of family-style restaurants, had built a
strong customer base with a simple strategy: high-
quality home-style cooking. But in 1986, Picadilly's CEO
suddenly decided to substitute mass-produced products
in the company's recipes in order to cut costs. The board
allowed the plan to proceed, despite its potential conflict
with Picadilly's core source of strength with customers.
The chief financial officer, James W. Bennett, questioned
why the company would change its proven recipes
overnight without so much as a test program. Receiving
no answer, he quit. Six years later, in 1992, with profits
and market share declining, the board fired the CEO and
brought Bennett back in his place. He quickly reversed
the recipe decisions and, with them, the company's slide.
The obvious question is, Why did the board allow the
previous CEO to change the business's core strategy
when the new plan was so clearly suspect?

The recent, very public crises at some of the largest
U.S. corporations reflect the same dynamics. At Westinghouse, by the late 1980s, there were clear internal warning signals about the company's aggressive move into
financial services: great risks were being taken by a relatively inexperienced divisional team. The move was
allowed to continue and expand until, in the early 1990s,
it blew up and dragged the company into disaster. Amer-

ican Express suffered several years of dismal performance in its core credit-card division before one director
brought the situation to a head by compiling a list of
management policy initiatives and shortfalls that had
gone unchallenged by the board while the business
atrophied.

At Borden, the board allowed a disastrous conglomer-
ation strategy to proceed throughout the 1980s despite
signs that the businesses being assembled were not
working together. At least 90 acquisitions had been
made during that period. Then the board brought in a
new CEO, Anthony S. D'Amato, to fix the problems.
D'Amato pursued a strategy of consolidation and
streamlining, but, over the next five years, he made many
missteps in implementation. The board waited until
shareholders were on the verge of revolt and then sacked
D'Amato and brought in Ervin R. Shames. But that was
not the answer. Borden's stock went into a free fall. The
board gave up and sold the company to Kohlberg Kravis
Roberts for less than $14 per share; three years earlier,
the company's stock had been at $30.

Cases of shareholder challenge and even of corporate
takeover illustrate that specific policies are what matter,
not the overall competence of CEOs, and that the real
problem with boards is an unwillingness to challenge
specific policy decisions. In the late 1980s, several
investors mounted an attack on Gillette, which was
undervalued by financial markets. A world power in the
consumer products market and shaving products in particular, Gillette was generating enormous cash flows but
had high costs and complacent managers. The company
fought off its challengers, and, in the process, its managers reevaluated many corporate policies. Following the
takeover attempts, CEO Colman Mockler cut costs and

restructured, and Gillette's performance soared. It remains strong under the leadership of a new CEO. The obvious question is, Why didn't the Gillette board prod Mockler to make those changes before? Insiders say Mockler and the board knew Gillette was undervalued but spent more time debating takeover defenses than questioning which policies were causing the valuation gap. In the managed corporation, boards do not prod managers when performance is not a disgrace.

Creating the Governed Corporation

Given the real problems that lead to corporate failure, what is to be done? The answer lies in creating a model of corporate governance in which the focus is not on monitoring managers but on improving decision making. The goal should be to decrease the possibility of mistakes and to increase the speed with which they are corrected.

The most important step is to involve directors and shareholders in decision making. Just as a democratic political system cannot work without involved citizens, corporate governance cannot work without the informed involvement of the three critical groups: directors should help managers make the best possible decisions, and major shareholders should be able to speak directly to senior managers and the board about what they think of corporate policies and decisions. Input from directors and shareholders can mitigate the behavioral problems that cause companies to cling to bad decisions. And it can open up decision

Three critical constituencies—managers, shareholders, and the board—must all have a voice.

making—fostering debate, bringing in better information, offering new perspectives, and reducing false consensus and insularity. With shareholders and boards involved in decision making, the corporation is *governed* rather than *managed* because the three critical constituencies all have a voice.

To create the governed corporation, companies must start by rethinking the role of directors. The board must be proactive—and effective—in the policy-making process. That goal requires a different set of board changes than the usual corporate governance reforms. Independent directors and CEO audits, for example, are not key because neither helps board members participate effectively in decision making. In fact, a myopic emphasis on independence may hurt board effectiveness by encouraging detachment rather than involvement.

Five broad areas of change are needed. First, board members must be expert. Directors must be well versed in the complexities of the company and its industry, of finance and financial structure, and of relevant law and regulation. Many boards have little aggregate expertise in the core industry or finance; such a board simply cannot be an effective partner in decision making. For example, in 1993, CalPERS CEO Dale Hanson asked IBM board members how many of them had a personal computer on their desks; the answer was none. How could such a board assess IBM's position in the PC market?

Second, board-meeting procedures should focus on debating new decisions, strategies, and policies, not just on reviewing past performance. That means running meetings differently. The bulk of agenda time should focus on new strategies and organizational change. New boardroom procedures should be instituted to encourage debate. For example, instead of a lead director, boards should consider appointing a designated critic for each major policy decision. That ensures that new policy proposals are evaluated effectively and makes criticism expected and acceptable.

Third, directors need better access to information— on products, customers' viewpoints, market conditions, and critical strategic and organizational issues. Typically, directors receive information packets shortly before meetings. If they are to be partners in decision making, directors must be empowered to seek out their own information from those in the corporation, and they should be required to get firsthand knowledge of the business. At General Motors, new board guidelines empower directors to ask anyone in the company for information. At the Home Depot, directors are asked to visit stores regularly to get feedback from customers and employees.

Fourth, directors should be required to devote a substantial portion of their professional time to the corporation. At many corporations, four to six board meetings per year is the norm—

Director compensation— usually $25,000 to $50,000— should be increased by about 500% and linked to stock performance.

hardly enough for meaningful involvement in decision making. At General Motors, directors spent an average of 24 days on company business in 1993. At Lockheed, another corporation with an active, involved board, there are ten full board meetings per year plus numerous committee and partial meetings.

Fifth, board members must have the right incentives. They cannot be expected to undertake the difficult task of formulating and challenging corporate policies unless real gains are associated with successful service. Director compensation—typically $25,000 at a midsize company, $50,000 at a large one—should be increased by about 500% and linked to stock performance.

Overall, the goal of the reforms is to make the board function not as a distant referee but as part of a team of decision makers. Shareholders should not want boards to be independent and distant, concerned only with their downside liability if the corporation plunges into disrepair. Instead, shareholders should want board members to feel dependent—not on the CEO, but on the company—for their own incomes and reputations. Directors should feel that their own personal fortunes hinge on their ability to create value through their service. Then they will be proactive in evaluating opportunities and correcting flawed policies.

Once board policies are changed, communication must be improved among managers, boards, and capital markets. Large outside shareholders—residual claimants on the corporation's long-term profits—are in an ideal position to render an outside second opinion on corporate policy. Boards and managers need to hear that opinion directly as a check on insularity.

Failure to consult major shareholders on important matters of corporate policy is equivalent to elected representatives failing to consult their constituents. Yet a survey of approximately 150 corporate chief financial officers that I conducted last spring indicates that few boards have direct knowledge of shareholders' concerns. When asked, "Does your board fully understand the concerns and viewpoints of your shareholders and of capital markets?" two-thirds said no. To the question, "Has your board made a significant policy decision that you knew to be counter to the interests of shareholders and detrimental to value?" half said yes. When asked, "Is your board failing to take actions that you believe the company should take to maximize value and performance?" half said yes.

Formal policies are needed to create a structured interaction among shareholders, boards, and managers. Several corporations, including IBM and Westinghouse, have created board-level committees on corporate governance to keep tabs on governance practices and the concerns of shareholders. Other companies, such as Lockheed, consult directly with shareholders about prospective policies, particularly those concerning capital markets, before they are implemented.

A promising area for direct communication among shareholders, managers, and the board is director nominations. For many decades, director selection has relied on the perspectives of corporate insiders—board members and managers. Yet directors are supposed to reflect the preferences and views of outside shareholders and hence outside markets. Several companies, including Lockheed, Beckman Instruments,

Governance reforms should be put in place before a crisis, when a corporation is doing well.

and Time Warner, have instituted a consultative process for director selection in which shareholders have suggested nominees and, in some instances, vetoed prospective candidates. The result is a process that does not deed shareholders any formal powers but allows them to give critical input informally.

The reforms that I have described can be developed by general counsels, CFOs, CEOs, and board members. The idea is to put them in place when the corporation is functioning and performing well, before a crisis arises. Crises signal a failure—a breakdown—of the corporate governance process. If boards, managers, and shareholders adopt procedures based on the governed-corporation model in good times, then when difficult issues arise, the dynamics of a well-governed corporation will prevail. The board will function as a team, shareholders will have input, and the company can make quick and relatively painless midcourse corrections rather than suffering decline and crisis.

Ten years ago—indeed, for the bulk of the twentieth century—corporate decision making could not have been reformed easily in the ways I have described. Shareholdings were small, and shareholders were dispersed and passive. Creating a model of corporate decision making that did not cede most of the power to the CEO was virtually impossible. But, as noted earlier, ownership has become increasingly concentrated in the past decade, and large institutional investors are motivated to protect their interests by influencing corporate policy. Public pension funds have been joined by private money managers in seeking both discrete policy changes and long-term policy involvement in portfolio corporations.

In 1994, the Investor Responsibility Research Center, a key monitor of corporate governance activity, noted:

> *Breaking with tradition, a number of large shareholders aggressively sought to guide corporate strategic decision making in 1994 by pushing for spin-offs and other restructuring moves aimed at unlocking share value. These efforts threaten to shatter the old corporate paradigm that splits corporate governance into three distinct areas of functional responsibility: shareholders elect directors; directors hire management and set broad corporate priorities; and management runs the company's day-to-day operations.*

At Sears, for example, shareholders pressed management to reverse its diversification into financial services and concentrate on its retail core; the company responded, and performance improved. In the fall of 1994, money manager Ladenberg Thalman, a significant shareholder of Conseco, raised concerns that the company's planned acquisition of Kemper Corporation would prove economically harmful. Conseco abandoned the acquisition attempt. At Chrysler, investor Kirk Kerkorian publicly exhorted management and the board to stop hoarding cash; the news of Kerkorian's suggestions sent Chrysler's stock up nearly 10%, and the Chrysler board responded with new financial policies.

The new, informed policy involvement of large shareholders is a necessary foundation for the governed-corporation model. But the true spirit of the governed corporation is not realized when shareholders instigate action and companies react. The governed-corporation model is achieved when corporations invite the participation of shareholders and strengthen internal decision making before problems occur, averting the need for contentious shareholder-initiated activism.

Governed Corporations and Corporate Renewal

The move from the managed to the governed corporation will come slowly and will not be pursued by all corporations. Such change can take years, especially at companies governed by individuals who have subscribed to the old philosophy for decades. Indeed, some executives will actively oppose the new way of viewing boards, managers, and shareholders. Consider the opinion expressed by one CEO in a recent interview in *Inc.* magazine: "I want only one thing from a board: compliance. Directors can make only one of two statements. It's either 'I agree' or 'I resign.' " Board members, too, can be resistant to change, particularly if they are isolated from the needs of the corporation and steeped in the old, conservative approach.

But many companies are moving in the right direction. As noted earlier, General Motors, The Home Depot, Lockheed, IBM, Westinghouse, Beckman Instruments, and Time Warner have already taken some steps toward becoming governed corporations. Another example is Bay Networks, which was created last fall, when Wellfleet Communications and SynOptics Communications merged. After the merger, the management team created a board of six individuals who have a great deal of computer and technology expertise. Each director received a package of new options, thereby giving the new board a stake in making the merger work. The board of Compaq Computer is also widely known for its expertise and the high level of involvement of board members in the corporation's policies and strategies.

None of those companies have fully realized the model of the governed corporation yet. But each represents progress—a growing recognition of the importance of board and shareholder involvement in decision making. Moreover, the number of different approaches shows that governance policies will, and should, vary according to organizational needs, leadership styles, and corporations' internal politics.

Some corporations have made great progress toward the governed-corporation model. Take Ceridian Corporation, whose core businesses are defense electronics and information services. Five years ago, the company—then Control Data—was on a financial precipice. Since then, it has rebuilt its business franchise, replacing an insular decision-making process with one that is participative and strongly connected to both board members and major investors.

At the end of the 1980s, Control Data, one of the first major computer companies, was among the most extreme manifestations of the managed-corporation model in the country. CEO William Norris made decisions autonomously. Often, those decisions appeared at odds with economic reality. Control Data had spiraled downward, and Norris had circled the wagons. As one insider put it, management spent far more time concocting takeover defenses than running the business.

Throughout that period, the Control Data board was shut out of the decision-making process. It did not question management decisions, and management would not have allowed it to. Once, in the late 1980s, the board's finance committee opposed a proposed acquisition. Management proceeded with the acquisition, and the finance committee was abolished.

By 1990, the company's performance had become so bad that its very survival was in question. Major institutional investors were pressuring the board to take action. Finally, it did. After a major restructuring, the current CEO, Lawrence Perlman, was put in charge. In 1992, Control Data downsized and became Ceridian. Perlman, who came to his position in part through the efforts of major shareholders, has a very different perspective from Norris's, which is reflected in how Ceridian is governed.

Ceridian Corporation's CEO has moved the board to center stage in decision making and actively sought shareholder feedback.

Perlman has moved Ceridian's board to center stage in decision making. Major questions of corporate policy—restructurings, capital-structure decisions, and overall strategic direction—are subjects for debate by the full board. Before major decisions, managers provide directors with extensive information and ask them to come prepared to criticize new initiatives. A recent capital-structure decision, for example, involved more than 200 pages of briefing material on industry practices and potential valuation consequences.

Ceridian has also been among the most aggressive companies in seeking a direct, ongoing dialogue with its major institutional shareholders. It seeks shareholder feedback both on overall corporate structure and on specific prospective policies. After the company spun off its computer operations and adopted its new name, Perlman invited the top ten institutional shareholders to attend a board meeting to talk about the newly restructured company. His aim in organizing the meeting was to promote understanding between board members and shareholders.

In 1994, Ceridian was contemplating the use of targeted stock to enhance its financial flexibility. Under the plan, the company would have issued separate classes of stock, tied to its separate businesses of defense electronics and information services. The plan offered additional capital-market flexibility. But Perlman also recognized that targeted stock is controversial among investors. So he raised the idea in general terms with some of Ceridian's top institutional shareholders. The response was not enthusiastic; in fact, no shareholder was in favor of using targeted stock. Shareholders were concerned that it would confuse the market and raise questions about which business Ceridian was most committed to for the long term.

Perlman reported the results of those conversations to the board. The board weighed a number of factors, including the positive recommendation of the company's investment banker and the negative views of shareholders, and decided not to pursue the targeted stock plan. One reason was shareholder sentiment. Board members and Perlman felt that pursuing a major policy initiative that the corporation's major owners opposed made no sense.

Ceridian operates in a highly competitive and uncertain industry. The policies just described do not guarantee that it will be able to beat its competition. But they have kept Ceridian in tune with its markets and reduced the risk of major mistakes in policy. From the restructuring to the end of 1994, Ceridian added more than $1 billion of market value for its shareholders. That is largely due to the fact that Ceridian is governed rather than managed.

The power and promise of the governed corporation are clear. Governed corporations have more robust, pluralistic, and adaptable decision-making processes. There are more new ideas. The oversight process is less personalized: it focuses not on the competence of the CEO but on the effectiveness of the organization. There is less risk that insularity, stasis, and false consensus will blind the organization and tie it to mistaken policies. The policies of the governed corporation make the organization accountable to its markets.

In the political arena, U.S. citizens recognize that an open decision-making process is an effective one. The same is true in corporate governance. Over the long term, an open, flexible process with involvement by boards and shareholders creates stability and lessens the likelihood of convulsive, contentious change.

The manager-centered, hierarchical process of decision making that has ruled U.S. corporations was the consequence of decades of dispersed ownership and shareholder passivity. The activism of large shareholders has laid the necessary foundation for a different approach. Policies that reintroduce shareholders and boards into decision making will create healthier, more self-renewing, and more flexible corporations.

The Limits of Economic Solutions

THE TAKEOVERS AND LEVERAGED buyouts of the 1980s present compelling evidence of the limits of the managed-corporation model of governance and of reforms whose goal is to strengthen that model.

Proponents of takeovers and LBOs argue that those measures increase market discipline and corporate efficiency. Takeovers are supposed to give shareholders the power to oust bad managers and replace them with good ones. LBOs are supposed to motivate board members and managers to create value by giving them large equity stakes.

But, often, those market mechanisms are not sufficient to improve performance. Witness RJR Nabisco, the $24 billion crowning jewel in Kohlberg Kravis Roberts's LBO empire. Leveraging RJR was supposed to improve its performance. But since the buyout, RJR has been caught in the shifting tobacco market and has made its own mistakes. Admitting failure, KKR in 1994 swapped most of its RJR stock to buy Borden, a troubled consumer-products company.

Why do such methods fail? Because takeovers and LBOs do not directly address the real problems in corporate governance. They change ownership structure and shift control, but they do not automatically improve decision making. If governance failures stemmed solely from bad managers and bad incentives, then takeovers and LBOs would always be the answer. But because governance failures hinge at least as much on behavior, personalities, and politics within organizations, changing ownership structure and incentives is not enough. At RJR, competitive complexities caught managers off guard. The benefits of the LBO did not offset the realities of the tobacco market.

Takeovers create the opportunity for new managers to control assets, which can sometimes improve performance and increase value. In addition, they are the right answer when combining assets can create synergy. But they also create a constant threat, leading to a war mentality among board members. Takeovers give boards an excuse for regarding the market as a threat and for turning inward, ignoring reality and disregarding the concerns of outside stockholders. Many takeover bids themselves represent flawed decisions by the acquirer.

LBOs create huge incentives for managers and board members by concentrating ownership in a small group at the top. In doing so, however, they also remove the corporation from the public market and scrutiny. If the new team begins to make bad decisions, there are no public shareholders who can press for change. Moreover, many of the LBOs of the 1980s created huge risks as well as huge financial gains. Many new managers and board members were forced to balance on a knife edge between wealth and bankruptcy. Some economists think such risks create incentives; common sense suggests they can just as easily lead to crisis.

A better approach to creating incentives is the relationship-investing concept. In that approach, one or more outside shareholders take substantial ownership positions—10%, for example—and form a relationship with the company, which sometimes includes board representation. The model brings an outside-shareholder perspective to bear on decision making; it also energizes the board. And, as long as the investor's stake is not too large, it allows other investors to have ongoing input. Indeed, in the best cases, the large investor acts as a channel between the smaller investors and the company—bringing their opinions before the company on their behalf.

The heightened incentives and aligned interests inherent in acquisitions and buyouts are not bad. But they will not always succeed by themselves. They focus on who is in charge rather than on how decisions are made. Perhaps their greatest weakness is their tendency to deter outside stimulus and change by locking up ownership and control. The biggest problem at most large companies is insularity and stasis.

In the model of the governed corporation, the goal is to open up the company to the outside market. The best solutions are ones that inject the opportunity for constant market feedback—without the constant threat of a change in control.

Originally published in March–April 1995
Reprint 95210

Appraising Boardroom Performance

JAY A. CONGER,

DAVID FINEGOLD, AND

EDWARD E. LAWLER III

Executive Summary

RARE IS THE COMPANY that does not periodically review the performance of its staff, business units, and suppliers. But rare, as well, is the company that does such a review of one of its most important contributors—its board of directors. Reviewing a board's performance is not an easy proposition: it has to be done by the members themselves, people who generally have many other responsibilities and whose time is always at a premium.

But done properly, appraisals can help boards become more effective by clarifying the individual and collective responsibilities. They can help improve the working relationship between an company's board and its senior management. They can help ensure a healthy balance of power between the board and the CEO. And, once in place, an appraisal process is difficult to dismantle, making it harder for a new CEO to dominate a board or avoid being held accountable for poor performance.

Done properly is the key here, though. Done incorrectly, board appraisals can degenerate into self-serving evaluations or unpleasant, time-wasting exercises. Worse, they can evolve into rigid mechanical processes that discourage innovation. In fact, all of the approaches the authors observed in two years of research were incomplete. The authors have therefore drawn on the strengths of several different approaches to synthesize a best-practice process that is both rigorous and comprehensive.

Rare is the company that does not periodically review the performance of its key contributors—whether they be individuals, work teams, business units, or senior managers. But one contributor usually escapes such review, and that one is arguably the single most important—the corporate board.

More than a few good reasons come to mind why companies should annually review the effectiveness of their boards, the most pressing of which is that influential investors—in particular, institutional investors—are beginning to demand it. A 1997 survey commissioned by Russell Reynolds Associates found that the quality of a company's board has now become an important evaluation factor for institutional investors.

Other important reasons abound. Appraising a board's performance can clarify the individual and collective roles and responsibilities of its directors, and better knowledge of what is expected of them can help boards become more effective. While no one can yet show a direct link between a board's effectiveness and its company's profits, few would be likely to disagree that improved board performance translates into better corporate governance. In fact, directors have told us that after they initiated board evaluations, their meetings went more smoothly, they got better information, they acquired greater influence, and they paid more attention to long-term corporate strategy.

Done properly, board appraisals may also improve the working relationship between a company's board and its management—a powerful argument in itself for doing them. Directors have told us that the evaluation process encouraged greater candor in their dealings with the CEO and other senior managers. Formal appraisals

Done properly, board appraisals may improve the relationship between a company's board and its management.

of the board as a whole, and also of individual board members and the CEO, help ensure a healthy balance of power between the board and the chief executive. Furthermore, once in place, the appraisal process is difficult to dismantle. Thus an institutionalized review process makes it harder for a new CEO to dominate a board or avoid being held accountable for poor performance.

The changing roles and rewards for corporate directors create another compelling reason to review board performance regularly. As greater attention has focused on corporate governance, directorships that were once relatively low-paid and essentially honorary positions have become demanding and well compensated. Investors understandably want to know what they are getting for the millions of dollars in stock options and cash their companies are paying to directors.

The most obvious impediment to periodic board evaluations is that no one can perform them but the board itself. However, if the right evaluation process is in place, self-evaluation need not be self-serving evaluation. Nor need it be the kind of unpleasant, time-wasting event that makes performance appraisal nearly every manager's least favorite activity.

Appraisals in the boardroom are a recent and not-yet-widespread phenomenon. A survey of directors at *Fortune* 1,000 companies conducted in 1996 by Korn/Ferry International indicates that even though roughly 70% of the largest U.S. companies have adopted a formal process for evaluating their CEOs, only one-quarter evaluate their boards' performance. Evaluations of individual directors are even rarer and more controversial, occurring in just 16% of the companies surveyed. (See the table "What Companies Evaluate.")

No one can evaluate a board but the board itself. Nevertheless, self-evaluation need not be self-serving evaluation.

Over a two-year period, we interviewed and gathered written surveys from CEOs and board members at a

What Companies Evaluate

Percentage of Fortune 1,000 Companies with Evaluation Practices

Type of Evaluation Practice	%
CEO	69
Whole board	25
Individual directors	16
CEO and whole board	23
CEO and individual directors	14
CEO, whole board, and individual directors	10

Source: 1996 Korn/Ferry Survey

dozen companies that are aggressive pioneers in performing and applying boardroom appraisals. Our research has allowed us to develop a set of best practices that represents a composite of the most effective techniques used by all these organizations.

Any discussion of performance appraisals must necessarily cover two broad areas—the *what* and the *how*. In the case of a board, what should be appraised is its ability first to define its responsibilities and establish annual objectives in the context of those general responsibilities, and then its record in achieving those objectives. An appraisal must also look at the resources and capabilities the board needs and has available to perform its job. The how of board appraisal is, of course, the process the board uses to evaluate its own performance. We'll discuss the what first, then the how.

Activities and Responsibilities: What the Board Does

There's little argument about the modern board's responsibilities. First, it is responsible for business strategy development: not for setting strategy—that job falls to the chief executive and senior management team— but for ensuring that a strategic planning process is in place, is used, and produces sound choices. Further, the board must monitor the implementation of current strategic initiatives to assess whether they are on schedule, on budget, and producing effective results.

Second, a board is responsible for seeing that the company has the highest caliber CEO and executive team possible and that certain senior managers are being groomed to assume the CEO's responsibilities in the future.

Third, as the ultimate oversight body, the board must be sure that the company has adequate information, control, and audit systems in place to tell it and senior management whether the company is meeting its business objectives. And it is also the board's responsibility to ensure that the company complies with the legal and ethical standards imposed by law and by the company's own statement of values. Finally, the board has responsibilities for preventing and managing crises—that is, for risk management.

Before a board can even begin to evaluate its performance in these broad areas of responsibility, it must articulate the specific actions that each of them implies. In other words, boards must set objectives for themselves within those broad categories against which they can eventually measure their performance. The boards of most of the companies we looked at create a set of objectives annually—generally speaking, at the beginning of the fiscal year—that reflects the directors' collective judgment about which aspects of the board's overall responsibilities need particular attention in the coming year.

The nominating or governance committee may design an initial set of objectives that it feels covers the essential responsibilities of an effective board. But it is vital that the full board and CEO then take time to discuss, debate, and agree to the final set of objectives and to establish priorities among them. Not until then can the board establish the criteria it will use to measure its own performance in meeting those objectives. For instance, as part of its role in developing business strategy, the board and the CEO may decide that the company will seek to become the leader in Latin America in its major product segments within three years. The board then specifies the evaluation criteria it will use to assess whether it is helping the company achieve that goal. Those criteria may include improving the board's knowledge of the region by adding a director who has Latin American expertise, facilitating the establishment of a partnership with the Venezuelan government, or holding a board meeting at the company's Latin American headquarters in Brazil in order to meet local managers.

Because of the many demands on a board's time, not every board responsibility need be evaluated every year. In a particular year, it is useful for the board to pick four to seven areas that it needs to improve. So, for example, a board might choose to focus one year on improving its evaluation of senior management talent at the divisional level, on identifying a system for tracking a strategic initiative, and on enhancing its CEO evaluation procedure. The choice of topics should reflect the areas the board feels are currently the most vital to the company, but all major areas of responsibility should be covered periodically. It is best if the board sets these developmental objectives in a meeting separate from the one at which the board appraises its performance during the past year.

Resources: What the Board Needs to Do an Effective Job

A board is a team of knowledge workers, and to do its job, the board needs the same resources and capabilities that any other successful team of knowledge workers needs. Research done here at the Marshall School of Business's Center for Effective Organizations indicates that to do their jobs effectively, such groups need *knowledge, information, power, motivation,* and *time.*

KNOWLEDGE

The combined knowledge and experience of the board members absolutely must match the strategic demands facing the company. Because today's business environments are so complex, it is nearly impossible for a single person or even a small group of individuals to understand all the issues that come before a board. Such complexity argues for assembling a group of members whose skills and backgrounds are diverse and complement one another. Ideally, so that the board not grow unwieldy, each of its members should satisfy more than one need. Selecting directors for a single area of expertise or background characteristic can contribute to the creation of a board whose members focus only on their particular interests.

The knowledge and experience of the board members absolutely must match the strategic demands facing the company.

A performance evaluation that systematically assesses boardroom expertise and identifies current and future gaps is therefore critical to assuring that the board maintains the right mix of knowledge. A leading aerospace company uses a simple matrix highlighting the capabilities of its directors, making it easy to see if individuals representing the right mix of knowledge are on both its board and its various committees. The required capabilities are derived directly from the company's long-term business strategy. They include competencies in such areas as developing new technologies, doing business in the Pacific Rim, dealing with governments, and creating shareholder value.

The CEO explains the matrix's purpose: "We use it to evaluate the disciplines we want to have on the board, the capabilities we currently have, the capabilities that may rotate off the board because of retirement or other reasons, and the types of people we should be looking for. We do the same thing with the composition of our board's committees. We want to make sure those committees have the right kind of breadth and that there is a continuity of experience. We try to move people around so that the capabilities we want to have on particular committees are covered. It's a chess game that gets played every year."

INFORMATION

To be effective, a board needs a broad range of information about the condition of its corporation. It needs, for example, up-to-date information on the competition, on key strategic issues, and on possible acquisition targets. And it needs that information presented clearly and concisely because its time is limited. Furthermore, the board needs to get its information from a broad range of sources such as outside stakeholders, customers, employees, and the directors themselves. An evaluation of board resources, therefore, must examine not only the kind of data a board gets but also their origins.

POWER

An effective board needs authority—the authority to act as a governing body, surely, and to make key decisions—but also the power to see that senior management is accepting and implementing its decisions. One clear way to grant the board the independence it needs to exercise effective oversight of the CEO is for the board's chair to be someone other than the CEO, to be someone who represents the owners of the company.

"This is the single most important factor in creating the right balance of power needed for effective governance," says Benjamin Rosen, chairman of Compaq Computer Corporation. "Our country has this separation of powers, why shouldn't companies?" The separation of chair and CEO is common in companies initially financed through venture capital. But it is unlikely to be widely adopted among large corporations in the United States because, Rosen says, "there is so much peer pressure on CEOs to keep the two roles together." Today only 3% of those chairing boards at large public companies in the United States are not current or former chief executives of the company.

Even when a single person is both the chair and the CEO, a company can take steps to achieve a balance of power between the board and chief executive. One step is to appoint a lead director, who represents the outside directors when setting agendas for meetings and who can take charge in a crisis. Instituting a formal evaluation of the CEO's performance also works to maintain a balance, as does making a portion of the CEO's compensation dependent on attaining targets agreed to by the board. (See "Evaluating the CEO" at the end of this article.) In addition, the board can schedule regular executive sessions at which only outside directors are present. These meetings would allow the board to discuss sensitive issues without raising alarms among senior managers.

A board's power is a function of the backgrounds of its members and the way they are chosen. It is crucial, then, that a committee of independent directors—and not the CEO—oversees the process of selecting new directors. Directors who have ties of business or family to the CEO and the company may have difficulty exercising independent judgment. They may be more easily swayed by the CEO's strong stance on an issue. Similarly, board members who sit on one another's boards create potential personal conflicts of interest.

It follows, then, that to assess the state of its own power, the board should in an appraisal ask such questions as: Do we have a healthy balance of power with our CEO? Is the board itself well led? Do we control the agenda of our own meetings? and, Can we act quickly to replace the CEO if necessary?

MOTIVATION

The right incentives must be in place to align directors' interests with those of the individuals they are meant to represent: the shareholders and other stakeholders in the corporation (employees, customers, and the community, for example). Together with the process by which directors are selected, the reward system is a lever that companies can use to influence the motivation of board members.

A growing number of companies require directors to own shares, paying them partially or wholly in stock rather than offering pension plans or other perks.

An evaluation process identifying high-quality directors may be as critical as compensation policies that motivate behavior.

According to David Golub, managing director at Corporate Partners, which specializes in taking large equity positions in publicly traded companies, "The most important factor in determining if a board is effective is whether there is a small group of directors—it doesn't need to be every one—that has a substantial ownership stake in the company, enough so that it hurts them personally if the company is underperforming."

The board evaluation should take note of the requirements for owning stock and the degree to which directors' compensation is in stock rather than cash. It should also examine the mix of short-term versus long-term rewards. Although it makes sense to orient directors' compensation toward the long term—with, for instance, options that can be exercised only after several years or upon retirement—it is also important to remember that money may not be a director's primary motivation. As Harvard Business School professor Jay W. Lorsch has recently commented, "Directors, most of whom are highly compensated in their regular jobs, do not serve for financial rewards. Rather, they join boards because of the new ideas they gain and out of a sense that they have a responsibility to participate in the governance process." Thus having an evaluation process in place that focuses on identifying high-quality directors and encourages an open exchange of information may be as critical as establishing compensation policies intended to motivate some desired behavior.

TIME

To make effective decisions, directors need sufficient, well-organized periods of time together as a group. Evaluations should note whether the frequency of meetings is adequate, whether there is sufficient time available to prepare for meetings and to deliberate on important decisions, and whether time spent in meetings is used efficiently. For instance, board members should not devote time in meetings to getting information from management that could have been communicated earlier. Rather, they should spend meeting time engaged in substantive discussion and decision making. Accordingly, an appraisal should consider whether board members are receiving the advance information they need in order to come to meetings prepared to debate crucial issues. It should also consider whether the meetings themselves are devoted to the right issues. Evaluating the way the board operates will not necessarily lead to the conclusion that it needs to meet more often. On the contrary, after appraising its own performance, one board we studied reduced the number of regular board sessions and instead delegated more work to committees and telephone conferences.

Because even the most efficient boards can run short of time for in-depth discussion of corporate strategy during regular meetings, some companies are scheduling annual strategy retreats. In some cases—for instance, in high-technology industries, where product life cycles can be less than a year long—meeting annually in such retreats is not enough. That's why Compaq devotes "a couple of hours at every board session to some part of the business that is going to affect its strategy," says outside director Ken Roman.

Dayton Hudson Corporation adopted a similar process after conducting an evaluation of its board. The directors concluded, says general counsel and corporate secretary Jim Hale, that "there's too much strategic information for us to absorb all in one blast. Spread it out over the year, and give us the strategic issues affecting one operating division at each meeting." The board evaluation process should help boards decide whether they currently have enough time to discuss strategy and what the optimum forum for strategy discussions should be.

Evaluation: How the Board Rates Itself

Whatever their individual advantages, all the approaches to board appraisal we observed were incomplete. Either they failed to gauge the adequacy of important board resources and capabilities or they failed to set clear performance objectives. We have therefore drawn on the strengths of several different approaches to synthesize a best-practice process that is both rigorous and comprehensive.

Self-evaluation is not an easy issue for any group to deal with. It is particularly difficult in the case of boards because it requires board members to make judgments and decisions about themselves and about issues that affect all stakeholders. The effectiveness of the evaluation very much depends on how the board structures the evaluation process. It should consist of three phases: The first—setting annual board objectives at the beginning of the fiscal year—we have discussed above. The process picks up again at the end of the year, when, in the second phase, the board secretary collects and disseminates information about the board's activities. With that information in hand, in the third phase, board members can judge how close they came to meeting their objectives while also examining the adequacy of the resources available to them over the year.

Evaluation is particularly difficult for boards of directors because it requires members to make decisions about themselves.

DISSEMINATING INFORMATION

The information disseminated to board members should come from both internal and external sources. It should include an analysis of how the board spent its time in meetings, breaking down the year's activities and accomplishments according to how they contributed to each area specifically set out for evaluation in the annual objectives. For instance, board members should be able to scan a list of topics and issues that they addressed at meetings the previous year relating to business strategy development, and the list should be organized by the dates of each meeting and the length of time spent on each topic. Wherever possible, this information should be linked to tangible benefits to the board or the company that may have resulted from these activities. For example, the record of a decision by the board to expand the company's markets in China should be connected to the opening of the company's sales office in Beijing some two months later and to sales figures in the region for the appropriate period.

A careful examination of the topics covered at board meetings might also reveal that certain of the board's objectives or portions of the company's business were largely overlooked. Such an analysis might reveal, for example, a failure to hear from a member of the senior management team who is a prime candidate to succeed the CEO, or perhaps it might reveal a failure to review the company's substantial real-estate holdings.

At the start of every fiscal year, Texaco's board defines its general areas of responsibility (for instance, oversight of the company's financial health, assuring adherence to corporate vision and values, planning for succession, and reviewing the CEO's performance) and lists, according to their priority, objectives it creates for itself within each broad category. At the end of each year, the nominating committee then analyzes the minutes of all board meetings to determine how the board allocated its time relative to those priorities. Board members receive this information as the basis for a discussion of the board's effectiveness. "We look back each year and ask how we did on each of these points and did we do enough," observes Texaco's corporate secretary, Carl Davidson. What results is not a report card, he explains. "It is, rather, an objective listing of what we spent time on and a subjective assessment of how well we did in paying attention to our key responsibilities."

An element essential to the board evaluation process was missing from nearly all the companies we studied: data obtained from outside the corporation. Information derived solely from internal sources may have inherent biases that distort the reality of the company's competitive or financial position. Outside data are particularly pertinent when assessing a board's performance relative to that of its competitors. Institutional investors, market analysts, regulatory bodies, the press, and academic journals are all potential sources of outside information. Evidence suggests that institutional investors, in particular, want to be asked for their views of board performance. Our analysis of the Korn/Ferry survey indicates that directors also view the evaluation process as significantly more effective when boards receive feedback from company stakeholders.

Evidence suggests that institutional investors, in particular, want to be asked for their views on board performance.

EVALUATING THE BOARD'S EFFECTIVENESS

After board members have had time to review the information provided to them, a lead director, the head of the committee overseeing the evaluation, or a respected and trusted outsider (such as the corporate counsel) should survey all board members confidentially to collect their views on the board's performance relative to the objectives it had set for itself and to examine the nature and adequacy of the available resources. The survey should use a mix of open-ended questions and numerically scored multiple-choice items that remain consistent from year to year, thus allowing the board to track its performance over time.

Amoco Corporation and Motorola take two different approaches that are both quite effective. Each uses a four-page questionnaire. Motorola's asks board members to indicate degrees of agreement or disagreement with 27 specific statements, such as: "The board of directors is prepared to deal with unforeseen corporate crises." It then poses seven open-ended questions, one of which, for instance, asks: "Does the board have an appropriate mix of overview and approval activities? If not, what should be different?" (For a sample of Motorola's questionnaire, see the exhibit "How Motorola Polls Its Board Members.")

The Amoco questionnaire summarizes the board's responsibilities in each of six categories ("succession, planning, and selection," for instance) and asks directors to judge the board's performance in each as "excellent," "satisfactory," or "needs improvement." In each category, there is also space for comment. Two open-ended questions at the end of the survey ask directors how they would rate the board's overall performance and solicit suggestions for improvements. At other companies, an individual member of the board—frequently, the chair of the nominating, governance, or compensation committee—conducts interviews with each director in person or over the telephone using open-ended questions. Written

How Motorola Polls Its Board Members

The following is the first page of a five-page survey that Motorola uses to evaluate its board of directors. The complete form includes 27 multiple-choice questions and 7 open-ended questions.

The following survey is a tool to help you think about the performance of the Board of Directors as a group. It is intended to enhance the Board's overall effectiveness. The results will be discussed at a future Board meeting. Please indicate to what extent you agree with the following statements concerning the functioning of the Board of Directors as a whole. Circle one response for each item.

The following questions refer to the Board of Directors

The Board of Directors:	Strongly Agree	Agree	Neither Agree Nor Disagree	Disagree	Strongly Disagree
1. has an appropriate level of involvement in CEO succession	1	2	3	4	5
2. has in place appropriate processes to assess the CEO	1	2	3	4	5
3. has sufficient information for CEO evaluation	1	2	3	4	5
4. spends an appropriate amount of time discussing the long-range future of the company	1	2	3	4	5
5. proposes changes in company direction	1	2	3	4	5
6. has a vision and a mission that is understood by all Board members	1	2	3	4	5
7. is prepared to deal with unforeseen corporate crises	1	2	3	4	5
8. has appropriate structures and processes to help evaluate company strategy and objectives	1	2	3	4	5
9. effectively inquires into major performance deficiencies	1	2	3	4	5

questionnaires yield more consistent information, and we believe they are equally effective as long as they include an option allowing directors to schedule an interview with the chair of the appropriate committee, if they wish.

The committee responsible for corporate governance should analyze and discuss the results generated by the evaluation data. At Honeywell, that's the nominating committee, which reviews the written questionnaires and comments from all board members. As at most of the companies we studied, the committee does so after the directors' names have been removed. Results are compiled into a single report showing nearly verbatim responses to each question, identifying where the board has met its objectives, and indicating where it needs improvement.

Finally, the committee's findings are presented to the entire board in summary form. The board discusses the areas identified for improvement and creates appropriate action plans. Not only is the content of the presentation to the board important but so is its tone. The presentation of appraisal results must be balanced, highlighting the areas where ratings or viewpoints diverge and preserving the anonymity of individual members unless individuals specifically ask that their names be used. The most effective presenters are those who are good listeners and are trusted by board members. They must be seen to be independent of the CEO and senior management. Lead directors are often a good choice. When the board has not appointed a lead director, a good choice is the outside director who heads the committee responsible for corporate governance.

Conducting an appraisal in this way has several advantages. First, the scores on the questionnaires help

the board members rank themselves objectively along a
series of dimensions. Directors can also see where their
viewpoints differ. But boards should also consider an
additional technique that we never observed, even in our
best-practice companies—having independent experts
on group process observe some board meetings and contribute advice on how the board's performance might be
improved. With little or no vested interest and an understanding of group-process issues, outside experts are better positioned to recognize dysfunctional team dynamics. They can also draw attention to implicit rules of
behavior that may be interfering with the amount and
candor of information flowing among board members.

Keeping the Process Effective

Once an effective board-appraisal process is in place and
running, it is a good idea to reexamine it regularly to see
how it can be improved or varied to avoid growing stale.
When Dayton Hudson, for instance, began evaluating its
board 15 years ago, it used a very formal process. Every
year, board members reviewed each description of the
board's responsibilities, as well as those for each committee, paragraph by paragraph, to determine whether
they were meeting their obligations. "There was a point
in our history when that was useful and productive,"
recalls the general counsel, Jim Hale. "But over time, it
got stilted, and we felt that it was more important that
we have good communication than that we have a specific format." Rather than serving as a forum meant to
foster rich discussion and debate, a board evaluation
that takes too detailed an approach can eventually turn
into a mechanical process in which accomplishments are
merely checked off. What's more, reviewing the same

dimensions repeatedly over many years will, at best, begin to yield merely incremental improvements and, over time, may discourage innovative challenges to established boardroom procedures. Using the same dimensions over and over again can also cause the board to lose sight of other areas it may need to review.

Throughout the last decade, Dayton Hudson's board has set aside a block of time each year to review its governance procedures and to evaluate their effectiveness, experimenting with a variety of different formats. Ideally, a board's governance committee will conduct a thorough review and critique of the board evaluation procedures, actively seeking input from all board members in the process. For example, during the takeover boom in the 1980s, members of Dayton Hudson's board did a case study to learn how the board of another company that had been through a hostile takeover dealt with that process. In other years, they have sent out written surveys to the directors, similar to the Amoco survey, asking them to assess the information the board was given and to suggest how the process could be improved. Last year, they circulated their extensive, publicly available, corporate-governance guidelines and asked the board whether any amendments were needed.

As the pressure mounts on publicly owned companies to improve their corporate-governance practices, we are likely to see more of them adopting formal board evaluations. A few will take the bolder step of formally evaluating the performance of individual directors. (See "Should Individual Board Members Be Evaluated?" at the end of this article.) But formal board evaluations are no panacea, particularly if companies are simply going through the motions to satisfy the investment community. The chair of one company that recently instituted processes for evaluating both its board and its individual board members admitted that he didn't believe it was important. "It's important to others, but it's not important to good corporate governance," he maintained. "It's just that people conduct best-practice surveys of corporate governance, and we wanted to have the evaluations on our checklist."

Even when employed at companies that do take them seriously, evaluations are no guarantee against trouble. Texaco's board has been a leader in the adoption of best practices in corporate governance, and yet these practices did not help it avoid a well-publicized incident suggesting corporate racism. On the other side of the coin, *Business Week* and *Chief Executive* magazines, for instance, consistently rate the Walt Disney Company as having one of the worst boards, as measured by governance procedure standards, and yet under Michael Eisner's leadership, Disney has produced exceptional returns to shareholders.

Boards are like fire departments: they aren't needed every day, but they have to perform effectively when they are called upon.

But if done correctly, evaluations create a way for the board and the CEO to hold each other accountable to clearly defined performance expectations while avoiding the dangers of getting the board involved in day-to-day management. Evaluations can also improve the operations of the board, clarify the respective roles of the board and the CEO, and ensure that both consistently focus on their responsibilities. Perhaps the clearest and most consistent benefit we've observed in those companies that have adopted board appraisals is a commitment by directors and the CEO to devote more time and attention to long-term strategy—and that by itself is an outcome significant enough to justify their implementation.

In a way, boards are like fire departments: they aren't needed every day, but they have to perform effectively when called upon. One chair observed that in good times corporate governance is largely irrelevant, but in bad times it is crucial. Formal, periodic board appraisals can help ensure that when the board is needed, all the right processes, procedures, members, and relationships are in place and ready to go.

Evaluating the CEO

FORMAL EVALUATIONS OF A company's CEO by its board of directors are becoming increasingly commonplace. The process should involve three stages: establishing evaluation targets at the start of the fiscal year, reviewing performance at midyear, and assessing results at the end of the year.

Just before the start of the company's fiscal year, the CEO and his or her direct reports should work with the board to develop the annual strategic plan establishing the company's short-term and long-term objectives. Finding the right objectives is a critical part of the process. Many companies have built their CEO's objectives and compensation package around annual financial objectives and the performance of the company's stock. Although essential, such measures fail to take into account such important responsibilities as the CEO's plans for his or her own succession, lobbying efforts, involvement in trade associations, efforts at internal communications, leadership skills, and success in labor relations. The most telling evaluations, therefore, include both financial and nonfinancial objectives. Still, our best-practice companies kept their lists to between five and ten objectives. In addition, it is a good idea to define carefully at least three levels of performance for each objective—poor, acceptable, and outstanding. These levels become the benchmarks for differing pay packages.

A common problem we have found is that boards rely too much on the CEO's self-evaluation. Self-evaluation is an essential part of an effective performance appraisal, but it is by no means sufficient by itself. Clearly, individuals being judged on their performance may have many reasons to be biased in the way they rate themselves. For example, one CEO admitted to us that he purposely lowers his self-evaluation, preferring to be "pulled up" by his board's evaluation rather than be "put down." We suspect that he is not alone. Self-assessment data must be balanced by other information. Ratings from customers and institutional investors, employee satisfaction surveys, and comparisons of the CEO's performance with that of leaders in-side and outside the industry are all useful sources of information.

Once the objectives are defined, the CEO must translate them into a set of personal-performance targets and specify how his or her progress will be measured against each. The CEO then shares these targets and metrics with a committee of the board—normally, a compensation or a board governance committee that ideally consists solely of outside directors. This committee makes recommendations to the full board, resolving any differences between the perceptions of the CEO and the outside directors regarding objectives. This committee also establishes the financial rewards that will result from meeting the targets. Committee members must collaborate with the CEO to ensure that targets are realistic but challenging. When the CEO and committee members agree on objectives and measures, the committee presents them to the full board for discussion and final approval.

Next comes the midyear review—which, like any midyear employee review, is a chance for the board to assess whether the CEO is on a course to meet or exceed objectives and, if not, to determine where the problems lie. The midyear review encourages directors to act before minor problems become major ones and ensures that the objectives as originally framed are still relevant. Such reviews may need to occur more frequently than once a year in industries where products and market conditions change rapidly.

The final stage of the CEO's evaluation should take place at the end of the fiscal year, when the board's compensation committee compares the executive's actual performance against the targets and determines the compensation it will recommend to the full complement of outside directors. Typically, this stage starts with the CEO completing a written self-evaluation that gauges his or her performance over the year. Individual outside board members should also complete a short questionnaire assessing the CEO's performance. We strongly recommend that the questionnaire combine open-ended questions with those that use a rating scale. Rating scales make it easier to compare different board members' evaluations and highlight clearly where perceptions vary. Open-ended questions allow people the flexibility to consider factors that fixed scales and targets may overlook.

The committee should also collect and consider pertinent outside information, such as perceptions of the CEO by the investment community and by its most valued customers. Using all this material as background, the committee should then prepare its recommendation, and the outside directors should meet to discuss and approve a final compensation package.

In many companies, the response to all of this information from outside directors to the CEO is oral and informal. Our research and our analysis of the Korn/Ferry survey data, however, indicate that directors consider the evaluation process more effective when board members give the CEO written feedback as well. Committing thoughts to paper forces deeper reflection and greater clarity. It also gives CEOs something concrete that they can review at their leisure after the meeting. Written appraisals also ensure that every director is heard—not merely those who are the most vocal.

Should Individual Board Members Be Evaluated?

PERHAPS THE MOST controversial issue in the area of board appraisal is the question of whether to evaluate individual directors. A survey of corporate governance conducted by Russell Reynolds Associates in 1997 showed investors feel strongly that boards need to be more aggressive in weeding out underperforming directors. Yet until recently, formal appraisals of individual directors have been relatively rare. Recent surveys by Korn/Ferry International and the American Society of Corporate Secretaries indicate that approximately 15% of large corporations assess the performance of individual directors. In our interviews of board members, we found overwhelming opposition and several concerns.

First, a number of directors and CEOs felt that turning a spotlight on individual members might undermine boardroom collegiality. They worried that it might drive away good board members who feel they have already proved themselves—and that would be a significant problem when competition to attract top directors is heavy.

Second, it is difficult to determine who should evaluate a director. Peers are one possibility, but they often lack the information needed to make an accurate appraisal of other directors' performance. Board members spend relatively little time together, and what occurs in the meetings may not be the best gauge of a director's contribution. Says one corporate secretary, "A lot of people are quiet [in board meetings], but they are very effective. They operate in different ways. It's what goes on in sidebar conversations, at dinners, during telephone calls between meetings, that kind of thing, that may really matter."

Third, since each board member brings a different set of competencies to the board, it can be dangerous to establish blanket evaluation criteria, which might, for example, overlook the different ways members contribute. And, finally, research on team effectiveness clearly supports the idea that when individuals are interdependent, as they are on a board, it is important to place the main emphasis on evaluating and rewarding the effectiveness of the group as a whole. Otherwise, people tend to optimize their individual performance rather than contribute to the effectiveness of the team.

But despite the problems with individual appraisals, we believe there is a definite role for them as one component of an overall board-evaluation process. Certain issues relating to the group's effectiveness simply cannot be addressed without evaluating individuals.

Although underperforming directors are relatively rare, it is a sound practice to identify them through formal assessments and to act quickly either to improve their performance or to remove them.

As the average size of boards decreases and the demands and rewards for serving on boards increases, companies need more from directors than good attendance and perfunctory questions. Individual evaluation is a good way to make performance expectations clear. Support for this view comes from our analysis of the Korn/Ferry survey data, which show that directors rate their board's overall effectiveness significantly higher in companies that do evaluate individual directors than in those that do not. (Even in those companies, however, evaluating the CEO and the entire board has a greater effect on directors' impressions of how effective their boards are. See the table "How Effective Are Evaluations: The Directors' View.")

Directors at Motorola recently began assessing themselves in response to boardroom discussions stemming from their full-board evaluation. Prompted by the question, What does the board add to the management of the corporation? the discussion turned quite naturally to, What does each individual member add? That led to an annual self-assessment exercise. Motorola's self-assessment questionnaire asks directors to indicate their degree of agreement (on a five-point scale) with 20 statements about their individual performance as directors such as, "I understand Motorola's industry and markets," and "I am fully prepared for board meetings." The questionnaire is for the individual's private use only and is not shared with any committee or other board member. It serves as a simple discipline and structure that directors can use to reflect on their own performance. It can also be used to start the transition to a peer-based evaluation.

Individual self-appraisal is not enough; individual biases reflected in self-appraisals should be balanced by the perceptions of others. One option is for the chair, the CEO, and the head of the board's human resources committee to meet periodically to assess each director

---

How Effective Are Evaluations: The Directors' View

Directors' View of the Impact of Various Evaluations on Their Board's Effectiveness

Significance of evaluating the following:			On the board's effectiveness in:
The CEO	The Board	Individual Directors	
Extremely significant	Significant	Significant	Governing, overall
Extremely significant	Very significant		Shaping long-term strategy
			Bolstering the company's image in the community
Very significant			Managing during a crisis
Extremely significant	Extremely significant		Planning for top management succession
Extremely significant			Anticipating possible threats to company survival
Extremely significant			Balancing interests of different stakeholders
Extremely significant	Significant		Monitoring strategy implementation
			Building networks with strategic partners
			Enhancing government relations

according to criteria similar to those Motorola uses. They should also use more objective criteria, such as the number of meetings the director has attended and the amount of the company's stock he or she owns. The results of that assessment can be given to the individual but not to other board members.

A company wishing to take a bolder—and potentially more effective—step could ask board members to evaluate one another anonymously. The most balanced approach is to combine anonymous peer evaluations with individual self-assessments and the evaluations by the CEO, board chair, or head of the human resources committee. The peer evaluations should be collected by a lead director, a trusted adviser, or an outsider who can provide board members with a summary of the comments and ratings of their peers. Keeping the source of all information anonymous, the adviser or outsider would then provide the full results to the committee charged with nominating directors to help it identify underperforming directors.

The results of individual appraisals are often the basis for developing a compensation program in which pay is tied to performance. In the case of directors, however, such programs are ill advised, as they pose too great a threat to board teamwork.

Originally published in January–February 1998
Reprint 98102

Changing Leaders

The Board's Role in CEO Succession

A Roundtable with Philip Caldwell, George D. Kennedy, G.G. Michelson, Henry Wendt, and Alfred M. Zeien

JAY W. LORSCH AND RAKESH KHURANA

Executive Summary

THE SELECTION OF CEO is one of the most important—and risky—events in the life of any company. Yet the way CEOs are chosen remains little discussed and little understood. The succession process has traditionally unfolded behind closed doors—some observers have even likened it to the election of a pope.

To shed light on what works and what doesn't in CEO succession, the authors lead a roundtable discussion with five distinguished corporate directors: Philip Caldwell, George D. Kennedy, G.G. Michelson, Henry Wendt, and Alfred M. Zeien. Collectively, the five directors have participated in dozens of successions, either as board members or as CEOs.

In a lively and frank exchange of views and experiences, the roundtable participants explore a broad range of questions: What can a company do to ensure a successful succession? How should management-development and succession processes be managed? How should the board work with the sitting chief executive during the process? What makes for a strong CEO candidate? When should outside candidates be considered? How much competition should be encouraged among potential CEO candidates? What role should executive search firms play? What role should the former CEOs play after they are succeeded? Their conversation illuminates a corporate challenge that is as difficult as it is important.

The selection of a CEO is one of the most important decisions a board of directors makes. Not only does a chief executive have an enormous impact on the fortunes of a company, but the very process by which the executive is picked influences the way employees, investors, and other constituencies view the company and its leadership. Choosing a successor often places a strain on the entire management team, especially when the new executive comes from outside the company.

For all its obvious importance, the way CEOs are chosen remains little discussed and little understood. The succession process has traditionally unfolded behind closed doors—some observers have gone so far as to liken it to the election of a pope. In the past, such secrecy was taken for granted. Today it is not. As the visibility and power of CEOs have increased in recent years, so too have the stakes in CEO succession. A variety of parties, ranging from institutional investors to Wall Street analysts to business reporters, are now scrutinizing those responsible for CEO appointments and the way in which the appointments are made.

The demand for greater transparency in selecting chief executives comes at a time when the role that the board plays in succession is changing in fundamental ways. It used to be expected that CEOs would choose their own successors and that boards would simply rubber-stamp the choice. Today the relationship between the board and the CEO has become more complex. In an age of takeovers, megamergers, and global competition, boards rarely have the luxury of passivity. They need to be active players in shaping companies, and one place where they are taking a stronger hand is in overseeing the entire succession process. It is up to the board to ensure that the process is rigorous, careful, and—perhaps most important—defensible.

With these broader changes as a backdrop, we recently led a discussion on CEO succession with five distinguished corporate directors. Collectively, the five have served on dozens of boards and participated in a score of successions, and most of them have been or are currently CEOs themselves. Drawing on their deep experience, the directors discussed an array of topics: the hallmarks of a successful succession process, the relationship between the board and the sitting chief executive, the characteristics of a strong CEO candidate, the considerations in choosing an outsider, and the use of executive search firms. Their conversation sheds light on an obscure area of management, providing other directors and executives with models for action.

Jay Lorsch: *A change in CEO is one of the most crucial events in the life of a company, and it is an event in which the board of directors plays a central role. Drawing on your experience as directors, how would you say that a board could best ensure a smooth and successful succession?*

Philip Caldwell: I would begin by laying out two assumptions. First, the best source of CEO candidates is the company itself. There are times when it will make sense to look outside, but in general you want successors to emerge from within the organization. Second, you want to have a choice of candidates—you don't want to narrow down to a single person too soon. With those two assumptions in mind, it seems to me that one of the board's most critical roles is to ensure the presence of an effective management development program for the

---

The Participants

Philip Caldwell succeeded Henry Ford II as CEO of Ford Motor Company in 1979 and as chairman in 1980. He retired in 1985, continuing to serve as a member of the board until 1990. From 1985 to 1998, he was senior managing director of Lehman Brothers. Currently, he is a director of the Mexico Fund, Mettler-Toledo, Zurich Holding Company of America, American Guarantee & Liability Insurance Company, Russell Reynolds Associates, and Waters Corporation. He is a former director of the Chase Manhattan Corporation, Castech Aluminum Group, Digital Equipment, Federated Department Stores, and the Kellogg Company, among other organizations.

George D. Kennedy is the former chairman and CEO of International Minerals and Chemical Corporation and of the Mallinckrodt Group. He also served as president of Brown Company and of Nationwide Papers. He is a director of Kemper Insurance Companies, Scotsman Industries, American National Can Company, and HealthShare Technology. He is a managing partner of Berkshire Capital Investors and a former director of Illinois Tool Works, Stone Container Corporation, and the Brunswick Corporation.

G.G. Michelson held numerous executive positions during her long career with R.H. Macy & Company and served on its board of directors. She retired from the company as senior vice president for external affairs in 1992. She

whole enterprise. While the CEO will be the person managing the program, the board needs to play an active oversight role to ensure that the program is in place and that it's working effectively. The program should be formally reviewed by the board at least annually.

George Kennedy: Phil, what would you say are the key elements of a good management development program?

Caldwell: It needs to be stable—you don't want to be fiddling with it constantly. It needs to be viewed as a fundamental element of the administration of the business. It needs to be well understood by everyone throughout the organization. And it needs to be comprehensive, forming the basic personnel program for the whole company. It should not be designed to cover just the very top layer of management.

---

is a director of the General Electric Company, president of the board of overseers of TIAA-CREF, and chairperson emerita of the board of trustees of Columbia University. She is a former director of many companies, including the Rand Corporation, the Irving Bank Corporation, Harper & Row Publishers, the Quaker Oats Company, Federated Department Stores, the Stanley Works, the Chubb Corporation, and the Goodyear Tire and Rubber Company.

Henry Wendt retired as chairman of SmithKline Beecham in 1994 after a four-decade career in the pharmaceutical, health care, and services industries. He is currently chairman of Global Health Care Partners and serves on the board of directors of Allergan, Atlantic Richfield

Company, Computerized Medical Systems, the Egypt Investment Company, West Marine Products, and Wilson Greatbatch. He is the author of *Global Embrace* (HarperBusiness, 1993).

Alfred M. Zeien recently retired as chairman and CEO of the Gillette Company. He was elected to those positions in 1991, after serving in a variety of international executive posts since joining the company in 1968. He continues to serve on Gillette's board, and he is also a director of BankBoston Corporation, Polaroid Corporation, the Massachusetts Mutual Life Insurance Company, and Raytheon Company. He also serves as a trustee or director of a number of nonprofit and educational institutions.

G.G. Michelson: I would recommend that it focus in depth on the top three tiers of managers. It should track their assignments, identify their development needs, and establish the career paths that will prepare them for higher responsibility. The board should be able to draw on information from the management development program to evaluate each manager in relation to the qualities that everyone has agreed are important for the successor CEO.

Henry Wendt: I agree about the importance of a strong management development program, but I don't think that management development and succession are necessarily synonymous. The board's supervision of the succession process should take place in the context of its broader responsibility for the organizational structure of the company, particularly the reporting relationships of senior executives. Those relationships, after all, define the routes traveled by the potential successors. At several companies on whose boards I've sat, I have insisted that the compensation committee's name be changed to the *organization* and compensation committee. That sends a very strong signal to everyone, including the CEO, that the board has the ultimate responsibility for the organizational structure as well as for the management development program and the choice of the successor. If the board doesn't keep a close eye on the structure, it will open the possibility that the CEO could manipulate the succession process.

Lorsch: *Can you talk a little bit more about how the board actually evaluates the candidates coming up through the organization?*

Kennedy: In addition to reviewing the information coming out of the development program, the board needs to have direct and regular contact with all the promising candidates. Some of the contact should be formal. For instance, you'll want to have the candidates make regular presentations at board meetings. But informal connections are also crucial. Board members need to take the time to get a feel for the personal chemistry of the candidates—to have casual conversations over dinner or lunch, for example. You have to have both formal and informal contacts to make sound judgments.

Wendt: Absolutely. You need both.

Michelson: I would add one ingredient. I think it's very important to try to establish situations in which you can see how the candidates relate to their peers. It's not enough just to look at how they act with the board or the CEO. I've seen talented executives who are very effective in their current jobs but who don't handle real authority well. It's hard to measure that capacity, but you can get a sense of it by seeing how individuals relate to their colleagues.

Caldwell: As companies have become more global, with managers all over the world, it has become harder to watch people in their everyday environment. But I agree that it's necessary. Both the CEO and the board should make it a high priority.

The Board and the CEO

Alfred Zeien: I think it's important that the board make sure the succession process begins about four years before the chief executive is expected to step down. It should require the CEO to clearly map out his or her plans for the process throughout that period. Four years gives you room to maneuver, and that's important. Let's say that a CEO looks out over the organization and sees that there's only one real candidate to succeed him. He's going to need to go out and bring new people into the top ranks of the company—to get the pool of potential successors up to three or four strong candidates. Getting those new people established and reviewing their performance takes time, so the board needs to insist that the process start early. And, to reiterate something that both Phil and Henry touched on, the board needs to prevent the CEO from steering the process toward one candidate. You've got to keep the options open.

Michelson: The board also has to make sure that the CEO feels comfortable changing his or her mind during that period. The candidate who looks best early in the process may not be the one who looks best later. It's often difficult for CEOs to admit they were mistaken, so it's incumbent upon the board to create a climate in which it becomes routine to reconsider opinions and points of view.

Kennedy: That requires good communication between the board and the CEO, which, as we all know, doesn't always exist. The board often fails to speak up, to challenge the CEO, either because it doesn't want to or because it's not organized to do so.

Wendt: Even when there is good communication between the board and the CEO, the chief executive may be too strong-minded to take guidance. He may listen, but he may not change. I can certainly think of a few examples of that.

Michelson: It is particularly apt to happen if the board is passive. Board members need to spend considerable time talking about the succession process, both with the CEO and among themselves.

Kennedy: G.G. raises a good point about the need for boards to talk without the CEO being present. That's not very common, but it's important. You need to have the opportunity to sit in executive session and talk frankly with your fellow board members about what's going well and what's not in the succession process, particularly concerning the chief executive's role. Those sessions should be a routine element of board meetings. Otherwise, the CEO may feel offended if he or she is suddenly asked to leave the room.

Wendt: I've been on boards where it was customary for the members to have discussions without the CEO, and those conversations were very helpful. We always designated one director to provide feedback to the CEO on any issues that came up in the session. Having a feedback mechanism makes the whole process less threatening to the CEO.

Kennedy: And more useful.

Wendt: Right.

Caldwell: But in creating some space between the CEO and the board, you need to be very careful that that space doesn't turn into a divide. The worst case is to have the relationship between the CEO and the board characterized by divisiveness or contention.

Kennedy: The board and the CEO have to remember that they have different roles. The CEO is the point person in the entire succession process—there's no question about that. But the CEO needs to understand that the board is going to make the ultimate decision on who the next CEO will be.

Zeien: I think in most cases the board would expect that the CEO would recommend a successor. At some point in the four-year process, he'll come forward and try to sell the board on the candidate he thinks is the best. For him to do that successfully, not only does he have to evaluate the candidates thoroughly and regularly, but he also has to keep sharing those evaluations with the board. He does not want to arrive at the end of the period and just say, "It's him" or "It's her." He has to have prepared the ground. And laying the groundwork is, of course, in his own best interest; otherwise, he's going to have a difficult time convincing the board that his choice is the right choice.

Wendt: I was once involved in a situation where that kind of groundwork was lacking. The CEO strongly recommended a candidate, but the board was deeply divided. About one-third of the directors supported the choice, another third were violently opposed, and the rest were on the fence. It became not just a succession problem but a problem of holding the board together and keeping the whole governance of the corporation intact.

Lorsch: *How did it turn out?*

Wendt: In the end, it worked out reasonably well, but it was a very threatening episode—the most dramatic internal crisis I've seen. I happened to be the chairman of the compensation committee, so I remember it distinctly. We had about a year before the CEO stepped down, and in the course of that year, the board met in at least ten serious executive sessions. It took a lot of discussion and debate, but the board held together, and we ended up choosing a candidate other than the CEO's. And, I'm happy to say, it was the right choice. I remain convinced that the CEO's choice would have been a disaster.

Avoiding a Horse Race

Rakesh Khurana: *We've talked about the importance of identifying several candidates—three or four was the* *number Al mentioned, I think. Do you want to encourage competition among that group, or do you want to minimize the competitiveness?*

Michelson: There will inevitably be competition, but too much is dangerous. If you turn it into an overt horse race, you'll lose a great deal of talent once the ultimate decision is made. A number of years ago, I witnessed a succession process that turned into a horse race—a long, public horse race—and the company ended up losing a lot of very good people. The company chose the right person in the end, but the process was much more painful than it needed to be. In a succession situation, you're probably going to lose good people whatever you do, but you'll guarantee a mass exodus if you make the competition too open.

Kennedy: Turning it into a public competition is unfair and unproductive.

Lorsch: *So far we've been talking about what I'll term a "natural transition," where the departure of the existing CEO is planned well in advance. Sometimes, though, chief executives leave unexpectedly—they may not be performing well, for instance, or they may get ill. They may decide that they can get a better job someplace else. What does the board do under those circumstances? How would the process change?*

Michelson: In emergencies, good management-development and succession processes become all the more valuable. If you have the mechanisms in place to monitor in-depth the performance of the next natural group of successors, you'll be well equipped to decide who ought to step in or to know that no one's yet ready for the post.

Kennedy: If no one is ready, you need to be prepared to bring in a caretaker—a person who takes charge for a period of time but who is not necessarily the succeeding CEO.

Michelson: Often, it will be an executive who's deeply experienced but is too advanced in age to act as chief executive for the long term.

Caldwell: Bringing in an interim CEO is sometimes necessary, but it's not ideal in my view. You should always try to have someone in the organization who could take over effectively as chief executive at a moment's notice. If at times you have to bring outsiders in to add depth to the top management team, so be it. It's best to have someone capable in the wings.

Zeien: On a practical note, you can do some things to prepare for such emergencies. I work on two boards where the CEO is required to leave with the head of the personnel committee a letter detailing what should happen if the CEO suddenly gets hit by a trolley car.

Michelson: When I chaired the compensation or management-development committees in a variety of companies, I annually asked the CEOs to designate someone who in their judgment should take over in an emergency. I did it every year because the CEO's view can change. And I always asked the committee and the board if they wanted me to open the envelope. Sometimes they did, and sometimes they didn't.

The Makings of a CEO

Khurana: *Most candidates for the CEO post will be heads of business units or other divisions. What does it take to move up from such a position to CEO? What qualities do you look for?*

Michelson: The qualities you look for in a CEO are different from those you look for in the leader of an individual business. A CEO has to have a strategic vision for the company. That's a hard thing to judge because business managers are rarely required to have a strategic view of the broader company.

Wendt: And a CEO has to be able to represent the company to outside constituencies, which is not something that business heads usually have to do.

Zeien: What's most difficult to gauge is how an individual will act once he or she is at the very top of the organization. As people rise through the ranks, it's fairly easy to track their accomplishments, to see how well they've worked with other people and how well they've formulated plans for their particular units, but those kinds of measures tell you little about how someone will respond to being in charge. I've seen very capable people who all through their careers have depended on the encouragement they receive from their bosses. Once they get into the corner office, there's suddenly no one there to pat them on the back. It's an entirely different kind of job.

Kennedy: I couldn't agree more. There's a mystery component that is really difficult to evaluate. All of a sudden, you've got a chauffeur and a limousine, you have an expense account that hardly anybody asks about, and you've got all kinds of temptations to let power go to your head. Whether or not a person will be staunch and sturdy enough to stand up to the temptations is a tremendous challenge for the board to judge.

Wendt: The CEO is often required to make very lonely decisions—there's a solitary aspect to the job—but the management development process tends to place a strong emphasis on team play. A great team player will not necessarily make a great CEO.

Lorsch: *If you're in a large, international company, I suppose you can gain a sense of how a person would respond to the top position by having him or her run a big unit that's distant from headquarters.*

Michelson: That can be helpful, but it's not foolproof. I've been in a situation where the CEO recommended a successor who had excelled at heading a big, distant business, and the board was unanimous in endorsing the choice. Yet when the guy assumed the top job, he didn't know how to handle the authority. He turned out to be overly autocratic, and we hadn't been able to foresee that.

Zeien: I've found that one way to gain insight into that mystery component is to pay close attention to how well the individual listens. When others are presenting information or expressing their points of view, is the person really listening to what they have to say, or is he just formulating his reply? Many of the problems that otherwise-talented people have when they become chief executives can be traced to their inability to listen.

Kennedy: Another thing that you have to look at is the candidate's personal stability, and that requires some knowledge of his or her family life and other activities outside the corporation. The better you know the person's sense of ethics and ability to put up with pressure, the better you can judge whether or not the person is going to be swayed by the power of the CEO office.

Choosing an Outsider

Khurana: *We've been focusing so far on successors who come from within the organization. But although most companies continue to pick insiders, studies indicate that about a third of new CEOs are now brought in from*

outside. What underlies this trend? And what are the
signs that an outsider might be the best choice for an
organization?

Caldwell: It used to be that a company was in one
kind of business and stayed in it. Today, companies are
much more likely to shift between businesses. We see
this dynamic at work in many of the mergers and acquisitions that have become so commonplace. A manufacturer may buy a financial service provider; all of a sudden, it's in a different business, and running that
business requires a different set of skills. The internal
CEO candidates may have been appropriate for the old
company, but they may not be right for the new company. A similar thing can happen when an organization
expands into new international markets, which also is
happening more and more these days.

Wendt: Even beyond acquisitions and globalization,
the overall pace of change in business is accelerating,
which puts pressure on companies to reinvent themselves. It can be very hard for someone within a company
to lead such radical change. It may take an outsider to do
the job.

Michelson: Another force at work is the increasing
mobility of managers. You can't count on people to be
lifers anymore. That means you're going to have more
turnover in the executive ranks, and as a result there will
be a smaller pool of natural internal successors.

Kennedy: For all those reasons, it's becoming more
politically correct to go outside. It used to be a no-no.

Zeien: In my view, though, it's still a sign of failure. If
you've established a good succession process, extending
over a full four years, you should have a worthy group of
successors in place.

Michelson: I agree. I'm a director of one company that will be facing a critical succession in a few years, and we have a strong set of candidates. As a director, I would be very embarrassed if we didn't have that kind of talent in place. I'd regard myself as having failed in my responsibility.

Wendt: But I'd go back to my point about the pace of change in business today. Even if you've done a good job grooming internal candidates, changes in the competitive landscape, in technological platforms, in the customer base—any or all of these—can sometimes create such profound dislocations that you have to rethink your criteria for a CEO. In those instances, you may have no choice but to go outside. The future of the company may bear little resemblance to its past or its present.

Michelson: But knowing such changes can happen, shouldn't you have been taking them into account throughout the succession process? Shouldn't the ability to cope with such challenges have been part of the criteria you've been using to evaluate candidates?

Wendt: That would be the ideal, of course. But in reality not all management development programs fulfill the ideal. There have been some great, great companies— IBM is a wonderful example—that didn't keep step with the pace of change. They've had to look outside their walls for their new leaders—and at least in IBM's case— it's worked out very well.

Khurana: *When you do go with an outsider, what is the effect on internal executives, particularly those who had been candidates for the top spot? When a company initiates a succession process, isn't it making an implicit promise to its top people that the next CEO will be one of them?*

Michelson: When you bring in an outsider, most of your best people will head for the exits.

Wendt: That's a real risk. It's much better to introduce outside talent into the executive pool before the CEO departs than to suddenly name an outsider as the chief executive.

Michelson: Now we're in full agreement, Henry. I would even say you should make it a formal operating policy to regularly seed the management team with outsiders. That helps prevent a company from becoming inbred, and it helps avoid the kind of abrupt cultural revolution you set off when you hire an external chief executive.

The Role of the Executive Search Firm

Khurana: *The question of outside candidates naturally brings us to the question of how executive search firms should or should not be used in the succession process. How do you see the role of a search firm?*

Kennedy: You ought to start with the understanding that you are better off if you don't need one. To expect an executive search firm to do the board's job is a miscalculation.

Michelson: But if you do need to use one, I've found that they're more helpful in the role of verifying qualifications and references than in identifying wonderful talent. A board's search committee can usually identify more good candidates than an executive search firm.

Kennedy: I have to say, though, that there are people in search firms who can open the door to candidates that otherwise would be likely to turn you down. There may be an executive out there who has been approached 35 times by different companies in the last year and has turned them all down, but the right search firm can sometimes get through and make the connection.

Wendt: A search firm can also help the board evaluate executive quality throughout the industry. As outside directors, most of us don't come from the industry that the company competes in. Working with a search firm can help us develop benchmarks of executive quality in the industry. That's often very useful.

Zeien: I've found that a search firm is only as good as the specification it receives from the board. We talked earlier about how difficult it is to judge a person's ability to assume the top spot in a company. Making that judgment becomes even more difficult when you're pulling someone in from outside. Most companies have distinct cultures—some almost look more like cults than cultures—and it's extremely hard to gauge how an outsider will fit in. The board has to develop a clear, detailed spec for the position—that's a role that it cannot off-load to the search consultant. The spec should guide the search and should form the basis for the board's ultimate decision. A good spec won't guarantee success, but it will certainly improve the odds.

Managing the Changeover

Khurana: *It can be tough for successful CEOs to give up their posts. Is there a danger that a CEO can end up staying on too long? And how can a board help prevent such a situation?*

Kennedy: I think your question again underscores the importance of establishing a clear, lengthy process for the succession—a four-year process, as Al suggested. That gives the sitting chief executive time to begin the

transition to a new life after the company, which can
indeed be a highly traumatic change. By establishing a
definite end point well in the future, you make sure that
the CEO won't suddenly get cold feet and start postpon-
ing his or her departure. Once the train gets started
down the track, it becomes very difficult for the CEO to
stop it.

Michelson: Establishing a mandatory retirement age
can also help provide a structure that ensures a smooth,
timely transition. I'm not saying it's right for every company and every board, but it's a practice that has served a
number of companies well.

Wendt: It's also useful to have an annual meeting
between the outside directors and the CEO where the
topic of retirement is discussed. You lay out the CEO's
timetable, the board's timetable, and you review the succession candidates. By having that discussion every year,
you help the process move forward to its natural conclusion on time.

Michelson: The board should also emphasize to the
CEO that one of the most important measures of his success is how well he handles the succession—not just by
preparing the next generation of leaders but by actually
moving aside to let them take over. Underscoring that
point can help a CEO realize the seriousness of the role
he plays in succession.

Zeien: It's worth noting that one of the great
strengths of the public corporation—the American-style
public corporation—is its formalized succession process
and the expectation that top executives will move on
when they're still at the height of their capabilities. You
don't find that in private companies, where founders
often never retire, and you don't find it in most universities or hospitals or governmental bodies. The U.S. public

corporation is unique in its assumption of a limited tenure for its chief executive, and I think that is a very positive thing.

Lorsch: *I think that brings us around to our last question. Should a retired CEO continue to play a role in the company?*

Michelson: While acknowledging that Phil Caldwell is an exception, I have to say that I believe in sudden death.

Wendt: I second that. The answer, in today's world, is no.

Michelson: In fact, I would say your successor is much more likely to come and ask your advice or get your opinion if you're not sitting on the board, if you've severed your formal connection to the company.

Kennedy: I once made the mistake of staying on the board after retiring as CEO, and I wouldn't do it again. An issue would come up for a decision, and the other board members would look to me as the former CEO and then look to the new CEO. The mere fact that they looked to see my expression—to try to gauge my feelings—was a terrible disservice to the new CEO.

Wendt: In two instances, I served as chief executive when the former CEOs were on the board, and it made things very uncomfortable. It's hard to propose changes without that being interpreted as a personal criticism of your predecessor. It's a terrible handicap.

Zeien: I'm not sure I'd say it never makes sense for the CEO to remain on the board. In some companies—Procter & Gamble, for instance—it's a tradition, and it seems to work for them. But one thing that I think is almost always a mistake is having the CEO move into a nonexecutive chairmanship. That doesn't work.

Kennedy: My feeling is that upon retirement the CEO becomes the exclusive problem of his or her spouse.

Lorsch: *George, I think we'll let that stand as the last word. On behalf of Rakesh and myself, I want to thank you all for spending time with us today. You've helped illuminate a corporate challenge that is as difficult as it is important. Thanks to all of you very much.*

Originally published in May–June 1999
Reprint 99308

Beyond Takeovers

Politics Comes to Corporate Control

JOHN POUND

Executive Summary

IN THE 1990s, politics will replace takeovers as the defining tool for corporate governance challenges, and a marketplace of ideas will replace the frenzied activity that dominated the financial marketplace in the 1980s. In the transaction-driven market of the past, corporate raiders used junk bonds and other financial tools to take control of their targets. In the new marketplace of ideas, debate will replace debt as active shareholders press specific operating policies for their target corporations in a new politicized market for corporate control.

John Pound, associate professor of public policy at the John F. Kennedy School of Government at Harvard, reports that investors are already using shadow management committees, independent director slates, and outside experts to influence management policy. Pound cites Carl Icahn's battle for control of USX as an example of the emerging trend. What began as a hostile takeover ended with a negotiated solution in which many constituencies ultimately played a role in the restructuring of the company.

This political approach to governance gives management a chance to embrace a bargain that is in its long-term interest. By promoting politically based tactics, managers can generate political capital with their major investors. Managers in companies as diverse as Avon and Lockheed now meet regularly with investors, seeking their input on both financial and strategic decisions. In the new politicized market for corporate control, striking a bargain with long-term investors is ultimately in the best interest of the corporation.

IN THE 1990s, politics will replace takeovers as the defining tool for corporate governance challenges, and a marketplace of ideas will replace the frenzied activity that dominated the financial marketplace in the 1980s. In the transaction-driven market of the past, corporate raiders used junk bonds and other financial tools to take control of their targets. In the new marketplace of ideas, debate will replace debt as active shareholders identify specific operating policies for their target corporations and then invent new mechanisms to get their message across to management.

In fact, investors are already using shadow management committees, independent director slates, and outside experts to critique management policy. These mechanisms allow investors to exert limited, rather than sweeping, pressure on management. Unlike the hostile transactions of the past decade, the new political mechanisms do not depend on the availability of financing. Nor do they depend on high-cost, all-or-nothing gambits aimed at achieving quick control, whether through tender offers or LBOs. Indeed, the new politics of corporate control have arisen precisely because these old approaches are no longer viable.

This new form of governance based on politics rather than finance will provide a means of oversight that is both far more effective and far less expensive than the takeovers of the 1980s. (See "The New Politicized Market for Corporate Control" at the end of this article.) Oversight based on a candid public discussion of corporate strengths and limitations will not be without contention; any serious debate about change is heated and sometimes bitter. But such debates are no different from those that occur in general elections and are entirely in keeping with the American vision of how large organizations should work. At their most vigorous, such debates are healthier and more sustainable than the quick deals of the late 1980s.

The USX Saga

The long and heated battle for control of USX, which took place between 1986 and 1991, serves as an excellent example of the changes taking place in the market for corporate control. What started as a hostile takeover attempt ended with a negotiated solution in which many constituencies played a role in the restructuring of the corporation.

In the early 1980s, once indomitable U.S. Steel was foundering in a newly competitive world market. Faced with the prospect of diminishing market share, the corporation made a decision to diversify—a choice common to many major U.S. companies at the time. In 1982, U.S. Steel bought Marathon Oil in the largest leveraged acquisition transaction to date. Four years later, the company continued its expansion into the energy field by buying Texas Oil & Gas, and it changed its name to USX as a symbol of its new hybrid status. By the end of 1986, over 70% of the company's $12 billion in revenues came from its energy division, and less than 30% came from its traditional stronghold in steel. USX was clearly headed out of its old business, into what managers hoped would be a more profitable environment in energy.

However, what management saw as potential new earnings in energy, the market saw as a dead end. The company's diversification attempt caused its shares to plummet, decreasing USX's market value by nearly 17%. On the heels of the Texas Oil & Gas acquisition, many large institutional investors sold their shares and complained publicly that USX was losing its direction and destroying value. In addition, the United Steelworkers' Union expressed fears that the debt taken on to finance the acquisitions would leave the steel business starved for cash and unable to compete in the world market.

By the end of 1986, the company's controversial acquisitions and impaired stock price attracted the well-known corporate investor Carl Icahn. In October 1986, Icahn announced his accumulation of an 11.4% stake in USX and made a $31 per share offer for the company. At most corporations, Icahn's offer would have led to a significant restructuring, an out-right sale, or a frenzied search for a white knight, but USX had adopted a series of stringent antitakeover devices and could afford the luxury of a "just say no" defense. The company simply refused to sell, and Icahn was stymied. The stalemate lasted over three years.

In the spring of 1990, a frustrated Icahn struck back, launching a novel proxy campaign. He nominated no directors and presented no threat to management. Instead, he promoted a nonbinding proposal asking USX's management to spin off the company's steel division to shareholders. The result was a hard-fought proxy contest that centered not on personalities, hidden agendas, or buyout plans, but on a single issue: the company's diversified structure. Both sides presented detailed arguments in favor of their position, and each side attacked the other's analysis. But because Icahn and USX management had earlier agreed to refrain from all extraneous legal action, the ensuing campaign was completely free of the costly and unproductive litigation that characterizes most proxy contests.

Ultimately, while management won the battle with 57% of the votes cast, Icahn won a number of converts to his agenda. Analysts and investors alike focused an increasing amount of attention on whether it made any sense to link USX's steel and oil operations. In the summer of 1990, the company appeared to be moving toward Icahn's agenda when it announced that it would place the assets of the steel company in a separate subsidiary, a move that would pave the way for some kind of structural separation of the businesses.

However, the move wasn't enough to satisfy Icahn. In November 1990, he announced the establishment of the USX Shareholders' Enhancement Committee, a group of 4 experts on USX's structure, strategy, and governance.[1] Icahn announced that he would fund the committee, providing money to communicate with shareholders and conduct analysis, but that otherwise the committee would be independent. From November through April, the committee would analyze USX and make proposals about its structure and strategy. If USX did not undertake a value-enhancing restructuring during that period, the committee would then run for election as 4 independent directors on USX's 15-person board. Icahn would have no representation on the committee or on USX's board if the committee members ran for seats on the board and were elected.

With the Shareholders' Enhancement Committee, Icahn took the political model he had pioneered one step further, invoking a mechanism that fostered an even more intensive and substantive debate over USX's strategy. The committee structure enabled the debate to expand from the limited four-week period prior to the annual meeting to a year-round campaign. By introducing a committee of independent individuals and an independent legal structure, Icahn distanced the debate even further from his agenda. The committee, funded by Icahn yet operating independently of him, constituted perhaps the first truly independent director slate in modern times.

In the ensuing months, the committee began communicating with a few of the company's major institutional holders. It retained counsel and drew up proxy materials. And it began independent research into the company's structure and strategy—a process without precedent in modern proxy campaigns. The committee engaged a set of expert labor economists and met with the president of the Steelworkers' Union to learn their concerns. It met with oil company experts to evaluate Marathon's strategy. It performed a detailed financial and strategic analysis of USX stretching back over a decade, comparing both operating and financial policies with those of its peers in the steel and oil industries.

At the end of January 1991, as the committee was ready to begin a process of broad shareholder outreach and meetings with management, the company announced a major and novel restructuring. Under the plan, USX proposed to issue separate classes of shares for its oil and steel divisions, while maintaining both divisions under one broad corporate umbrella. Each division would be run separately to maximize its value as a stand-alone entity. Shareholders in each business unit would have the ultimate say in any disposition of corporate assets—such as sales, mergers, or restructurings. USX would begin issuing financial reports on a stand-alone basis, as if the businesses were formally severed into two separate legal entities.

The committee, USX, and the Icahn organization agreed to a settlement where by the committee's activities would end and all parties would support the restructuring plan. Shareholders approved the plan at the annual meeting, and it was implemented at the end of May 1991. Since then, USX's separate financial reporting has begun to clarify what the committee knew early on: U.S. Steel is among the best run steel businesses in America. However, the numbers also confirm what the market feared: in the years following its acquisition by U.S. Steel, Marathon's performance deteriorated notably. By the late 1980s, it was under performing many of its industry peers. Remarkably, the committee's work and USX's separate financial reports confirm the market's original reaction to the Marathon and Texas Oil & Gas acquisition. Indeed, they give new credence to the common wisdom that managers seldom do as well running diversified industries as they do in their core businesses.

The USX saga chronicles the gradual eclipse of traditional, market-based takeover mechanisms in the late 1980s and the rise of new, political tactics in the corporate governance arena. By promoting a broad debate over USX's structure and strategy and by appointing an independent committee to conduct that debate, Carl Icahn succeeded in provoking corporate change where traditional corporate control mechanisms had failed.

The events at USX illustrate not only the different processes involved in the political model but also the different results. Icahn achieved a large portion of his goal but not all of it; USX did not engage in a legal separation or even create separate boards of directors for the two companies. To some observers, steeped in the take-no-prisoners dynamics of takeovers, this may seem like the worst possible outcome: nobody won a decisive victory. But viewed from a different perspective, precisely the reverse conclusion is suggested: everybody won. Carl Icahn ultimately achieved an important element of his agenda, but management continued to control the company. The year-long process, which took place without lawsuits, millions of dollars in fees to investment bankers, or the assumption of debt, represents a gradual and politically sustainable mechanism for corporate change. Such a result would have been unthinkable in the mid-1980s. It is intrinsic to the new shape of corporate control.

The Makings of Change

The fundamental shift toward tactics based on politics and substantive debate has been precipitated by a unique confluence of two trends in the governance arena. The first is the broad-based public backlash against hostile takeovers and debt-based financing. This backlash and the resulting collapse of the take-over market have created a pressing need for a new approach to governance. The second development is the rise of institutional investors, which creates a unique opportunity for active shareholders to influence corporate policy.

Many observers have noted the increasing concentration of ownership among institutional investors, but few have understood how their presence has changed the political dynamics of the marketplace. Wells Fargo Nikko Investment Advisors, the largest U.S. index fund, currently owns approximately over 1% of the top 1,000 U.S. corporations. So does the California Public Employees Retirement System (CALPERS). At the largest U.S. companies, a 1% holding is a huge investment that gives institutions an enormous incentive to become informed, involved owners. Some observers mistakenly believe that a 1% investment doesn't give an institution the incentive to act as an owner. But precisely the reverse is true. This ownership structure creates a simple but overwhelming economic incentive for informed behavior.

Consider an institution that holds 1% of the common stock of Mobil. The market value of this holding is over $200 million. Now consider the decision this holder faces when voting on a corporate issue. There may be the potential to gain or lose 20% of value—which amounts to $40 million—depending on the initiative's outcome. Moreover, simply selling could cost as much as $2 million. The 1% holder of Mobil shares, therefore, has an economic incentive to spend hundreds of thousands of dollars, if necessary, to analyze the issue. The sheer size of this stake and the trading costs associated with selling make the institution "captive." For large investors, it is cheaper to become informed and attempt to change corporate policy than it is to sell.

Now let's consider this from the standpoint of an active investor. A heavy concentration of institutional investors greatly lowers the costs of pressing an alternative agenda. Thirty years ago, appealing to a majority of shareholders meant circulating materials to tens or even hundreds of thousands of poorly informed individual owners. Now a dissident investor can reach the fiduciaries in charge of voting a majority of outstanding shares through a series of quiet phone conversations and private meetings with 25 informed investment professionals, all of whom understand the issues and can devote a significant amount of resources to analyzing them. This means that a dissident investor should be able to press a serious counter agenda with a controlling fraction of shareholders for much less than the $2 million to $5 million associated with a full-control proxy contest—in some cases, for as little as $250,000 to $500,000.

This radically changes the governance process. It opens the possibility of undertaking far more informal initiatives with lower expected gains than could ever have been undertaken in the past. If a proxy contest costs $2 million to run, then the sponsoring shareholder must have a large stake and an expansive reform agenda in order to recover his or her investment. But if a proxy initiative costs less than a half-million dollars, an investor can take a relatively small stake, circulate materials, and benefit when the price of the stock goes up just a few points.

For outside investors seeking to press a case against management, the informed position of institutions also means a greater opportunity to make a sophisticated case. Dissident investors can make arguments about optimal investment policies, research and development, or the mechanics of product distribution, and the informed and professional portfolio managers at leading institutions will listen, understand, and respond. As a consequence, rather than engaging in mass communication with a huge number of uninformed shareholders, active investors can convey a message about corporate policy to a small audience of sophisticated professional investors at a relatively low cost.

The Strengths of a Political Approach

The new political approach to governance thus draws its strength from both the collapse of takeovers and the rise of informed institutional investors. The former creates the need for active investors to develop new approaches to influencing corporate policy; the latter creates a class of owners who can and will respond to a political, substantive approach. The result is a system that has two broad strengths compared with corporate governance in the 1980s.

The first strength is the ability to address corporate operating problems directly—by proposing operating solutions. This may seem like the obvious purpose of a governance system, but it is not what prevailed during the past decade. Throughout the 1980s, clear and persistent operating problems led not to changes in operating policy but to changes in control through transactions such as leveraged buyouts or takeovers. (See "The Long History of Hostile Takeovers" at the end of this article.) Underlying virtually every major takeover bid of the past decade was a mistaken management strategy or decision. Lockheed had announced its intent to diversify into nondefense businesses where its expertise was questionable; USX had bought a series of oil properties that the market saw as not being effectively managed; Polaroid's margins were shrinking, and it had made a series of unprofitable product developments; Norton had lagged in market development.

The obvious response to these types of operating problems is a shift in operating strategy. However, in the 1980s, these kinds of operational problems generated financial solutions instead. Leveraging a company or buying it and acting as a broker by selling the pieces to other managers who will correct previous mistakes involves high transactions costs—including enormous fees to investment bankers and lawyers—and the potential for self-dealing. More to the point, financial solutions do not solve or even address the underlying operating problems but, rather, they create incentives for new managers to fix the old problems.

The leveraged buyout of Stop & Shop grocery chain is a good example of the drawbacks associated with promoting financial solutions to fix operating problems. Before it was restructured, Stop & Shop was making two mistakes. First, it was diversifying into geographic areas the company was unfamiliar with. Second, it was repositioning its Bradlees stores into a market segment where it had no competitive advantage. Despite the company's profitability, the stock market recognized these mistakes, and the company's share price began to fall. The low stock price attracted an active investor who controlled the Dart Group Corporation, and Kohlberg Kravis Roberts & Company then stepped in as a white knight. Along with the company's management, KKR took the company private in a dramatic leveraged buyout.

If there had been some way of reversing Stop & Shop's two bad operating decisions without changing the management and the whole financial structure of the company, everyone but the investment bankers and lawyers would have been better off. If Stop & Shop's mistakes were to recur today, they would not invite a hostile takeover bid. Instead, they might well prompt the establishment of an expert committee or a campaign to elect a minority of directors to the company's board. Either of these initiatives could correct management's operating policies without the imposition of a new and unnecessary financial structure, the displacement of management and workers, or the transaction fees and leverage associated with the deal that actually ensued.

Economists have argued that the great advantage of LBOs, such as the Stop & Shop deal, is that they avoid a confusing and inexpert public debate by boiling everything down to a simple price per share. That may have been an economic necessity in the era before concentrated institutional ownership. But it spells political disaster. Which brings us to the second critical advantage of the new approach to governance: its political sustainability and consonance with basic American popular values.

Americans have always had a deep distrust and political intolerance for pure finance, and the transactions of the 1980s stirred the populist pot of suspicions to an unprecedented degree. LBOs and other takeover transactions were based on secrecy, speed, and surprise. They eschewed due process and public debate. They imposed wholly financial solutions, including bust-ups, leverage, and recapitalizations. Driven by entrepreneurs with little political exposure, the deals were structured to accomplish the maximum restructuring in the minimum amount of time. In a matter of weeks or months, they imposed a huge new financial burden on the target corporation, while removing it from all public accountability. However positive the bottom-line results, to many, this process represented the ultimate arrogance of financial entrepreneurs.

The new politics of corporate governance stand in sharp contrast to the old ways of doing business. At the core of the new movement is a substantive discussion and debate over corporate policies. The new initiatives embrace due process and demand public debate. Change will be incremental, aimed at operating issues, and will occur relatively slowly, due mainly to the political conservatism of the major institutional investors. These changes have the potential to tilt the balance of public and political opinion in favor of active shareholder oversight for the first time in several decades because they create a system that holds corporate management accountable to the same kinds of rules to which Americans hold their public officials accountable.

The Critics

The newly political and institutionally dominated landscape of corporate governance and corporate control is not without critics. Managers level two charges against the emerging politicization of corporate control. First, they argue that the new tactics will promote short-termism by major U.S. corporations. They contend that institutional investors, anxious for quarter-to-quarter results, will push for extreme policy shifts that lead to short-term increases in value. But this criticism is only a variant of an age-old charge. In a previous incarnation, these same managers argued that this insatiable desire for short-term gain led to the takeover revolution. But in neither case has the short-termism charge ever been supported by empirical evidence; indeed, most research suggests that institutional investors are not driven by short-term results.[2]

The second charge leveled by managers at the new politicized tactics is that, in a politicized environment, every major management decision is open to second-guessing and every investor will want to voice dubious ideas about optimal corporate policy. Moreover, critics say some investors will use their ownership position to push noneconomic agendas—such as social and environmental issues—but the facts suggest that such initiatives, should they arise, are unlikely to succeed for two reasons.

First, institutional investors are extremely sensitive politically and, as a result, many are very conservative. This conservatism was first noted in the 1950s and is still evident in many institutions' current voting policies.[3]

In addition, a competitive marketplace disciplines bad ideas and ultimately eliminates them, just as a competitive market for takeover bids disciplined and eliminated uncompetitive bids. In the marketplace of ideas, the currency for exchange is credibility. As observers of the American political process, we all have a deep intuitive understanding of how this disciplinary mechanism operates. Centrists offering serious solutions to difficult national problems are given a hearing. Fringe ideas and candidates are quickly purged from the system.

A similar reputational market is already beginning to operate in the governance arena. Market players who repeatedly offer bad ideas, frivolous suggestions, or off-center initiatives will find that their influence wanes over time. Institutions will not support them, and corporations will—rightly—mount vigorous counteroffensives.

We are already seeing a natural evolution in institution activism that shows how the marketplace of ideas ultimately promotes efficiency. Five years ago, some public funds that wanted to be active in corporate governance launched contentious shareholder proposals on governance matters. The targeting of these proposals was at times random; they showed up with equal probability at top- and bottom-performing corporations.

Today the leading public funds are abandoning the shareholder proposal mechanism. Instead, CALPERS, the huge California pension plan, has isolated a dozen under performing companies and is engaging in quiet talks with management. Last year, CALPERS, the New York State Common Retirement Fund, and the Connecticut State Treasurer's Office proposed incremental changes in board policy to a large number of corporations. By mid-December, over two dozen corporations had agreed to institute the proposed policy requiring that the nominating committees of their boards have a majority of outside directors. These companies included Liz Claiborne, American Greetings, Dayton Hudson, Deere, and EG&G.[4] Without proxy activity—and without even a public announcement—these funds instigated changes to enhance long-term efficiency. This evolution represents market-guided learning at its best.

Examples of New Political Mechanisms

Throughout history, the innovative skills of expert intermediaries have created new vehicles for corporate control that are optimal for the times. In the 1950s, a new class of professional proxy solicitors—notably D.F. King and Georgeson & Co.—developed sophisticated new campaign techniques designed to woo tens of thousands of individual shareholders. In the 1960s, investors and investment banks honed the uses of the hostile tender offer. In the 1980s, a few maverick financial institutions, led by Drexel Burnham Lambert, invented a new form of debt financing that vastly increased the power and scope of the tender offer.

A new set of intermediaries will apply that same kind of innovative energy to the new political mechanisms of the 1990s. The following examples show just the beginning of a trend that will see many new mechanisms tested in the coming decade.

SHAREHOLDER COMMITTEES

When individuals still held a majority of corporate shares, informal committees of shareholders were a common part of the corporate landscape. Major stockholders would pool their resources and voting power, organizing to examine troubling management policies. They would not press a specific voting agenda, but rather would exercise a more informal, ongoing form of oversight.

Currently, there is a resurgence of this activity. Shareholder-sponsored policy committees, such as that established by Carl Icahn at USX, can act like a shadow cabinet in a parliamentary system, offering shareholders independent analysis and an alternative agenda. Or shareholders and management can co-sponsor a committee to give shareholders input. In 1991, at Baltimore Bancorp, a dissident investor ran on a pledge to establish such a committee and won. The new board has now established a shareholders' advisory committee comprised of the company's largest institutional investors. This committee gives shareholders an unprecedented guarantee, unthinkable even a few years ago, that the new team will be monitored to ensure that it keeps promises made during the proxy contest.

Similarly, Avon has set up a regular series of meetings among outside directors, major investors, and management, including the CEO, to discuss operations. In this form, the shareholder committee is less attuned to developing and publicizing a broad alternative agenda and more focused on evaluating new corporate initiatives.

DIRECTOR NOMINATING COMMITTEES

In traditional dissident proxy battles, the dissident investor chooses directors who are usually viewed as his or her surrogates. In the institution-dominated market, dissidents genuinely committed to soliciting independent board members can convene a committee of major stockholders to choose the best possible candidates. The dissident can then pledge to support a slate of candidates assembled by this nominating committee. This creates a true two-party corporate election where a dissident slate develops an alternative agenda and runs an independent campaign offering shareholders a distinct choice.

DIRECTOR NOMINATING PETITIONS

A simpler and less expensive version of the director nominating committee is the director nominating petition. A dissident shareholder, unhappy with corporate performance, identifies several new candidates for the board with clear expertise in the corporation's industry. He or she then circulates an open letter to other major holders explaining the importance of putting new directors on the board. However, he or she does not nominate these directors but, rather, petitions holders to submit the names of the candidates to the corporation's nominating committee, asking that they be considered for nomination through the usual corporate channels. If a large percentage of shareholders sign this petition, it creates significant political pressure to nominate and elect these directors. This message is conveyed, however, without ever submitting a nomination or soliciting proxies and thus fosters a different dynamic—one that is more political and less overtly hostile than a traditional proxy campaign.

ISSUE CAMPAIGNS

In situations where there is a clear and simple alternative to management's present policies, campaigns in which dissident investors press a specific alternative corporate agenda could become prevalent. Some issue campaigns result in a voting referendum on a competing business plan. In other instances, issue campaigns involve nothing more than continual lobbying by the dissident holder, without ever realizing the ultimate threat of a vote. These lobbying campaigns disseminate expert reports detailing corporate performance and arguing for specific new strategies. Dissidents canvass shareholders using sophisticated polling techniques to determine which issues are of broad concern to a large portion of the ownership base. These issues are then incorporated in the dissident agenda. This type of outreach has already occurred. At Lockheed Corporation, for example, dissident investor Harold Simmons included a number of significant shareholder-suggested proposals in his campaign platforms.

FRIENDLY MONITORING

Institutional investors, particularly public pension funds that are politically constrained from overtly hostile initiatives, will continue to hone their oversight policies. Many will develop sophisticated techniques for isolating under performing companies in their portfolios and devise structured ways of exerting influence at the worst-performing companies. A shareholder, for example, hires an independent consulting firm to offer strategic and financial advice to the under performing company. By designating such an intermediary, the institution brings expertise to the situation, yet maintains distance from the corporation.

The Corporate Response

In every previous era of corporate control, the development of new mechanisms has bred a frenzied and intense corporate search for protection. In the 1950s, for example, corporations instituted new voting procedures to protect themselves from proxy fighters. In the mid-1980s, corporations seeking shelter from takeover bids enacted poison-pill plans, engaged in scorched-earth defenses and leveraged recapitalizations, and adopted dual-class voting rights plans that provided management with absolute veto power over unwanted acquisition bids.

The same response is possible, even predictable, to the new, politicized corporate governance tactics of the 1990s. It is easy to envision charter and bylaw changes that would make it difficult to nominate minority director candidates and to establish shareholder committees. However, such a response would be a mistake; political oversight is ultimately in the corporation's best interest.

At no time has corporate America had a more natural long-term constituency than in the era of the institutional investor. All the characteristics of institutional investors—their concern about substance, their astute judgment, their political visibility, their intrinsic conservatism—make them open to overtures from corporations. Corporations that make even a minimal effort will build long-term relationships with their major shareholders and create a new kind of political capital that can ultimately lead to greater stability.

Because institutions are informed and engaged, corporations building bridges with their major investors will also create an early-warning system. By listening to the views of their largest investors, corporations can spot broad market concerns before they attract an active investor and provoke an initiative from the outside. By taking a systematic, indeed a scientific, approach to divining the concerns of their major institutional investors, corporations can create a governance process that begins to approach the ideal articulated for over a century by legal and economic theorists. In that system, the capital markets reflect the investors' broad expectations for the future. Those expectations are channeled back to the corporation through the market. By responding to these expectations, the corporation can adapt long before a series of obvious disasters in product markets or operating results spur a painful retrenchment.

The idea is not, as some CEOs have simplistically and defensively protested, that senior management should spend the year on the road talking to and placating major institutions. Instead, companies should institute formal mechanisms for obtaining investors' views. One possibility is to survey major investors for a detailed appraisal of corporate policy and direction.

A few corporations have bravely begun to undertake these types of experiments. In November 1991, for example, Lockheed announced a stock repurchase program of 4 million shares. Input from institutional investors was a key factor in Lockheed's decision to purchase the shares with free cash flow as it became available, rather than incurring new debt. Lockheed's open communications with investors have generated enormous benefits, including widespread understanding of Lockheed's policies and the creation of a good deal of positive political capital with the largest shareholders.

The emerging political approach to governance gives management a chance to embrace a movement that is in its long-term interest. Management attempts to deter this new approach would create a vacuum in the area of corporate control. With the torpor in the financial markets and the broad political and legal backlash against more extreme, market-based mechanisms, deterrence of an incremental approach to governance would leave investors with no tools to influence corporate policy.

The resulting lack of oversight would not last. In eras characterized by a complete absence of investor initiatives, political suspicions alight squarely on the shoulders of incumbent management. This antimanagement backlash has already arisen in the brief lull in corporate governance activity in 1990 and 1991. Executive salaries, perks, and power have occupied front-page headlines the way that Carl Icahn's and Sir James Goldsmith's exploits did just a few years ago. Without a revived market for investor oversight, top management will continue to stand trial.

Thus, to the degree that management isolates itself completely from the new breed of political shareholder initiatives, it will make itself a political scapegoat. In contrast, by promoting politically based, incremental oversight tactics, incumbents can generate an image of accountability and certify that they are indeed answerable to shareholders through an explicit, public process. This will turn down the political heat and ensure that there arises little social or political demand for more extreme, indeed retributory, means of oversight and accountability. By giving up a little power, corporations can gain an implicit guarantee of continuity and protection against more extreme threats.

The Appeal of the New Politics

To some observers, the legacy of the 1980s is mainly a financial one—manifested in the bankruptcy of Drexel Burnham Lambert, the imprisonment of Michael Milken and Ivan Boesky, and the retreat of corporate raiders. But seen in a broader context, the real legacy of the 1980s is political. For a decade, a series of corporate control devices imposed vast and sudden changes on major corporations. Yet faced with wrenching, disruptive change or no change at all, the American public has opted for no change at all. A popular and political uprising ended the hostile approach to governance that was out of step with American social preferences. Everyone involved now stands discredited to some degree: Wall Street for its greed; managers for their sloth; and raiders for what is perceived as a predatory search for assets and callous disregard for the social costs of their transactions. The result is political and economic paralysis.

Ultimately, the biggest victims of this vacuum are corporate managers, who lose the economic signals they need to remain ahead of the curve and to stay competitive. Corporations need oversight and managers need to hear and respond to signals about changing market conditions and broader social concerns.

The new politics of corporate control offer everyone a way out of a very difficult dilemma. They offer a sustainable middle ground between no governance and governance of the kind that was so thoroughly rejected in the 1980s.

By fostering an open, decentralized process and a full debate of alternative ideas, democratic politics will force corporations to evolve in response to changing economic conditions and changing markets. But democratic politics also place limits on the pace of change. Hence, the political approach to governance can prevent the divergence between the "short-term" financial solutions of the past decade and "long-term" corporate needs. Change is not sudden, but neither is it allowed to take decades.

A political approach also admits the interest and concerns of all constituencies—indeed, it is designed to assure that diverse interests are represented. It therefore provides an avenue for labor to propose an employee stock ownership plan, for example, or for community activists to actively pursue their claims as stakeholders.

This is the appeal of the new, politicized governance process. It is an open process in which a variety of groups can vie for support and press their message. It is a system that can give corporations great credibility. It is a process that offers a workable solution to the traditional American dilemma of financial action or inaction. It is a political solution to what has become a political problem, and it is a system that Americans will support because it is in tune, perhaps for the first time, with the dictates of the American governance ideal.

The New Politicized Market for Corporate Control

IN THE PAST FEW YEARS, there have been many situations in which political mechanisms, substantive debate, and compromise have ultimately replaced more traditional market-based corporate control mechanisms. The following examples represent an unmistakable trend toward a more politicized market for corporate control.

Lockheed. In 1990 and 1991, dissident investor Harold Simmons waged a year-long campaign at Lockheed. Simmons presented a detailed business plan for the corporation and, in conjunction with leading institutions, proposed several reforms to its governance process. In response, Lockheed's management took the unprecedented step of seeking input from leading institutional investors about Lockheed's board structure and composition. At the suggestion of major investors, the company appointed four new directors. The campaign accomplished two broad goals of the Simmons group: it made the company more responsive to its major shareholders and caused Lockheed to dump its plans to diversify.

Sears. In 1991, shareholder activist Robert Monks waged a campaign for a seat on the board of Sears, Roebuck & Co. Monks held only 100 shares of Sears stock, a signal, he argued, that he was not a traditional "raider" but simply a representative shareholder. He did not win but received the support of several large institutional investors. In response, the company announced that it was investigating several major restructuring options and moving aggressively to cut costs. Recently, the company agreed to add three new outside directors to the board by 1994, to expand the size of the board's nominating committee, to appoint an outside director as chair of that committee, and to exclude directors from serving as trustees of Sears's profit-sharing funds. Pressure on the company continues. In January of this year, Monks announced his intention to run once again for a seat on the Sears board. In addition, a group of employees of Sears's Allstate Insurance unit proposed their own director candidate and suggested that the company retain an investment bank to investigate the divestiture of Sears's financial and insurance operations.

Cleveland-Cliffs. In early 1991, money manager Julian Robertson became increasingly disenchanted with the performance of Cleveland-Cliffs Inc., a large producer of iron ore pellets. Robertson believed management was keeping an excessive amount of cash in the corporation to engage in what he expected to be an unwise capital investment program. He had 5 independent directors, unaffiliated with his organization, run for spots on Cleveland-Cliff's 12-person board. He vowed that all 5 nominees would be independent and that his sole goal was to ensure a new expert evaluation of management's policies. With the backing of Cleveland-Cliffs's major institutional investors, all 5 Robertson nominees won.

Avon. In 1990 and 1991, an outside investor group, Chartwell Associates, waged a fight to influence management policies at Avon. The battle began as a traditional proxy fight and ended with a series of compromises among dissident shareholders, management, and major institutional investors. The dissident group took two seats on the Avon board, and the company established a new policy to solicit the input and views of its major institutional holders. Institutional investors now meet regularly with Avon's CEO and members of the board to review and comment on Avon's progress in meeting its broad goals.

Diversified Industries. In early 1991, a partnership representing a Swiss investment company announced a 5% holding in Diversified Industries and indicated in its SEC filings that it might seek representation on the board. It then took the unusual step of forsaking an immediate proxy challenge in favor of a series of substantive negotiations with management. As a result, the investment partnership was awarded half the seats on Diversified's board. There was no proxy campaign and no expenditure of resources on unnecessary and divisive confrontations.

XTRA. In 1990, Robert Gintel, president of Gintel Funds, a Greenwich, Connecticut mutual fund, became exasperated with the poor performance of XTRA Corporation, a Boston truck and railroad leasing company in which Gintel had a major holding. Convinced that management had to be replaced, he ran a proxy contest for control of the company, winning an unprecedented 72% of the vote. The XTRA contest was unique both because it was the first modern proxy contest for control run by an otherwise passive mutual fund and, even more so, because its success was based on Gintel's timely response to concerns voiced by major institutional holders during the campaign. Early on, major holders questioned whether Gintel had an alternative plan for XTRA. In response, he proposed a replacement CEO and suggested a series of specific policy changes. Since winning the contest, Gintel has followed through on his pledges by establishing XTRA's first capital budget and substantially improving corporate performance.

The Long History of Hostile Takeovers

MANY MANAGERS THINK of hostile takeovers and proxy fights as an invention of the 1980s. There is, however, a long history to battles for corporate control. The term "company raiding" was first coined almost 100 years ago in the robber baron days of the late 1800s. Even then, historians tell us, it carried negative connotations. In those days, the term was often linked with images of watered stock, rigged markets, and stolen company assets.

In the mid-1950s, takeovers once again became the focus of public attention, only this time, the raiders were often seen as the good guys fighting bloated and wasteful corporate managements. The New York Central

Railroad, Montgomery Ward, and Industrial Brownhoist were all involved in hotly contested proxy fights. These takeover wars, launched before the invention of the modern tender offer, were political. Dissident investors ran coast-to-coast proxy campaigns, speaking at rallies, giving radio interviews, and exhorting millions of dispersed shareholders—and ultimately the public at large—to act to rectify the shortcomings of major corporations.

In the midst of these battles, the July–August 1955 *Harvard Business Review* ran "Thinking Ahead," describing managers' reactions to the takeover attempts. Much of what Harvard Business School professor Charles M. Williams wrote still rings true:

"How have professional managers viewed the operations of takeover groups? In such operations, the incumbent management is expendable. As a result, when control is in doubt, managers are in a quandary. Should they fight or concede defeat and attempt to salvage their jobs by joining up with the new controlling group? If they try to salvage their jobs under the new group in control, they may soon find they have to take orders that are distasteful or quit. In many instances, they have no choice about resigning, since new controlling groups often bring in their own people, particularly for top positions. Tradition is expendable to newcomers, who typically bring a hard economic, unsentimental approach to the business and its activities. . . .

"Professional management realizes that such results are almost inevitable in takeover operations. Add to this realization their equally natural resentment against the domination of the company's affairs by 'money men from Wall Street,' and the unsavory aspects of some of the takeover leaders, and you have a rather clear picture of why management generally has a jaundiced view of the 'takeover' groups. By and large, the public has much the same attitude of resentment and distrust. The public sees long-familiar patterns upset by strangers out for a financial killing. . . .

"I do not share this common reaction of management and the public. To me, it is much too narrow and too undiscerning. Management generally can gain much of value by reflecting more carefully on the significance of takeover operations. This is not to argue that *some* of the takeover groups do not deserve the label of 'unscrupulous pirates'—and public disdain as such. . . . But unsavory aspects of some elements in the opposition groups should not obscure basic points of significance in these situations:

"(1) I would argue that management has an obligation to do much more than just 'run the business.' It has a basic obligation to create values for the stockholders, to exploit fully, not just tolerably, the opportunities to use its capital and organization for the owners' financial benefit.

"(2) Management should be concerned with creating values in the short run as well as the long. It is not enough to take the point of view expressed recently by a prominent corporation president: 'We don't care what our stock is selling at; we are building values into the company, and someday they will be apparent in the market values.' . . .

"In my view, a significant number of managements have lost their concern for the stockholders. They have lost their 'zip,' their willingness to change, and their imagination. By their actions and attitudes, they have virtually forced revolution from without.

"Today in the United States, there are revolutionaries well armed with economic intelligence, monetary strength, and ruthlessness. This situation presents real challenges to management. Can it prevent the creation of opportunities for takeover groups? Can it supply the vitality, the imagination, and indeed the *internal* spirit of revolution that is necessary to achieve full economic progress in this changing world?"

Notes

1. The committee members were Darius Gaskins, former CEO of Burlington Northern and former chairman of the Interstate Commerce Commission; Ronald Gilson, Helen Crocker Research Scholar and professor of law at Stanford University; Katherine Schipper, professor of accounting at the University of Chicago; and John Pound.

2. See, for example, "Do Institutional Investors Destabilize Stock Prices: Evidence on Herding and Feedback Trading" by Josef Lakonishok, Andrei Shleifer, and Robert Vishny, Working Paper, University of Chicago, 1991.

3. In the 1950s, it was often noted that some types of institutional investors, such as banks and insurance companies, voted overwhelmingly for management in proxy contests. See, for example, coverage of voting in the Montgomery Ward contest in "Proxy Warfare May Create Tighter Governance Rules," *Nation's Business,* July 1955. For modern evidence on institutional voting behavior, see J. Brickley, R. Lease, and C. Smith, "Ownership Structure and Voting on Antitakeover Amendments" and J. Pound, "Proxy Contests and the Efficiency of Shareholder Oversight," both from *Journal of Financial Economics,* March–April 1988.

4. Data from the Investor Responsibility Research Center, Washington, D.C.

Originally published in March–April 1992
Reprint 92206

Redraw the Line Between the Board and the CEO

PERSPECTIVES FROM THE EDITORS

Executive Summary

THE AGE OF THE EMPOWERED board of directors is
here. Major public corporations now acknowledge that
they have no choice but to make management more
accountable to shareholders and that strengthening the
hand of outside directors is the logical means for doing
so. But exactly how to proceed remains an open question. More specifically, directors and managers wonder
how the relationship between the board and the CEO
should be recast.

Most directors and managers agree that the board
should be a more effective watchdog without undermining management's ability to run the business. They also
say boards need to decide how to distance themselves
more from their CEOs without turning a constructive relationship into an adversarial one.

187

Five corporate leaders—John G. Smale, Alan J. Patricof, Sir Denys Henderson, Bernard Marcus, and David W. Johnson—share their views.

"The board is responsible for the successful perpetuation of the corporation. That responsibility cannot be relegated to management."

—JOHN G. SMALE,
GENERAL MOTORS CORPORATION

"The success of the nonexecutive chairman arrangement is heavily dependent on the chairman's relationship with the CEO. If the chemistry is not good, the relationship isn't going to work."

—SIR DENYS HENDERSON, IMPERIAL CHEMICAL INDUSTRIES AND ZENECA

"How can outside directors constructively review management's strategy if they don't have a deep knowledge of the business?"

—BERNARD MARCUS, THE HOME DEPOT

T HE AGE OF THE EMPOWERED board of directors is here. Virtually all major public corporations now acknowledge that they have no choice but to make their managements more accountable to their shareholders and that, in general, strengthening the hand of outside directors is the logical way to do so. But exactly how to do so remains an open question. And, specifically, directors and managers wonder how the relationship between the board and the CEO should be recast.

Most directors and managers seem to agree that the objective is to make the board a more effective watchdog without undermining management's ability to run the business. They also say boards need to figure out how to distance themselves more from their CEOs without turning a constructive relationship into an adversarial one. In trying to strike a balance, directors and CEOs are debating several fundamental questions. They include:

- What role should a board dominated by outside directors play in formulating and reviewing the company's strategy?

- What rights should outside directors have to obtain information on their own, bypassing the CEO?

- How should boards evaluate management, especially the CEO?

- How does a board ensure that its members have the expertise to judge management's performance?

- What are the advantages and disadvantages of splitting the board chair's and the CEO's jobs between two people instead of entrusting them to one person?

In the following articles, five corporate leaders who have been grappling with these questions share their views. The perspectives of Alan J. Patricof, Sir Denys Henderson, and Bernard Marcus come from interviews conducted by HBR.

JOHN G. SMALE *is nonexecutive chairman of the board of General Motors Corporation.*

As the policies of corporate boards of directors get more attention in the investment community, in corporate-management circles, and in the business press, the General Motors board finds itself in an unexpected spotlight. The guidelines on corporate governance that our board adopted a year ago have drawn more attention than we anticipated. Our board did not develop them with any intention to "lead the way for corporate America" or "to shift power to the outside directors" or "to take stronger control over management," as some media interpretations have suggested. Rather, the guidelines represented a formal recording of the way we had been interacting with management for the past couple of years. For the most part, they were a codification of decisions the board had already made about how it should conduct its own affairs.

Because the subject of corporate governance is important to the larger business and financial communities, and indeed to society as a whole, I'd offer some personal views on the GM guidelines and why the principles on which they are based (if not the guidelines themselves) might be relevant for other directors and other companies.

First, I should emphasize that the guidelines are not etched in stone. They will undoubtedly change in the future. Nor are they intended to be a complete code of corporate governance. They work in concert with the bylaws, the certificate of incorporation, and the policies adopted by the board and its committees.

Furthermore, the GM board holds no conviction that all its guidelines are necessarily appropriate or relevant for other companies. Some of our ideas may be right for other businesses; some may not. We certainly do not see ourselves as universal arbiters of corporate governance. We were doing only what we thought was right for General Motors.

In my opinion, what is relevant to other companies about the GM guidelines is the fact that they exist at all. Their existence formally recognizes that the board of directors is separate from the management of the company—and that the board has separate and specific obligations to the owners of the business.

The board's basic responsibility is to see that the company is managed in a way that serves the owners' interest in successfully perpetuating the business. It has to act as an independent monitor of management, asking the tough questions that management might not ask itself. This needs to be done continually, not just in crisis situations but also when the company is doing well. I see this responsibility as active, not passive. The board's independent members, the outside directors, are uniquely capable of carrying it out. Being removed from management and not carrying the bias of a company's past success and its culture, they are able to help management by bringing different perspectives to the problems the company faces.

What is relevant about the GM guidelines is the fact that they exist at all. Their existence recognizes that the management of the company is separate from the board.

The GM board does not involve itself in management decisions, and the guidelines don't change that. The management team led by Jack Smith has full authority and responsibility for the day-to-day operations of General Motors.

With those fundamentals in mind, I'd like to offer some personal views on a few of the principles embodied in the GM guidelines, which I believe will enable a board of directors to function in a way that will meet its responsibilities best.

There should be a clear majority of outside directors.
On the General Motors board at present, the chief executive officer is the only inside director; all other members are independent and are not GM employees. While our guidelines provide us with the flexibility of having additional inside directors, it's quite clear that a board can't function as an independent auditor of the company's management activities if the majority of its members are also members of that same management. In my view, inside directors are essentially pointless for governance purposes; they simply are not in a position to speak out with independent insight about the company's or the management's activities.

A retired CEO should be considered an inside director because of his or her close involvement with the company's past success and its culture. Potential directors who provide significant services to the company, such as executives of law, accounting, or consulting firms, could pose conflict-of-interest problems; if such persons are on a board, they also should be considered inside members.

The independent directors should select a lead director. Currently, I have that role on the GM board as the nonexecutive chairman. But the lead director could be the chairman of one of the board committees if the board chairman is the CEO or an inside director. Also, the position could be rotated periodically among directors.

It is important to recognize, however, that every board member is equal. The lead director should not be a "first among equals"; rather, the person holding the job should serve as a facilitator of the governance process and the board's activities. For instance, this is the person who would chair the periodic meetings of independent directors and prepare the agenda for those meetings.

In addition to the routine or official meetings of the full board, the independent directors should meet alone on a regularly scheduled basis. Such executive sessions, which should allow enough time to ensure full and deliberate discussions of the performance of the business and the management, can be important for coalescing the board's interests and focusing its attention on specific areas or problems.

If there is no established schedule for independent directors' meetings, management could view such meetings as a threat simply because they would be extraordinary—something out of the normal context. The GM board has three scheduled executive sessions a year. The CEO participates in portions of them.

The independent directors should take responsibility for all board procedures. The board should establish its own policies, practices, and procedures. It should determine its size and its committee structure, whether there should be term limits, and what the retirement age should be. It should decide such matters as formats, time allocations, and agendas of meetings. Such decisions should serve the needs of the board, not management.

The GM board has a practice of rotating committee assignments and chairmanships at about five-year intervals. This practice tends to broaden the participation of the directors and bring new perspectives to the committees.

The GM board has had 14 members for the last few years, and we consider that to be about the right size. It is large enough to achieve a diversity of desirable experiences and backgrounds and small enough to function efficiently. But the number can fluctuate; we want to be able to add members when attractive candidates are available.

The board should have the basic responsibility for selecting new director candidates. It should be responsible for identifying and recruiting candidates for directorships, based on management's, as well as its own, evaluation of the skills, expertise, and characteristics required at the time. The CEO should be included in the process to ensure that management's insights and needs are considered. But the key point is that the board itself, not management, should be accountable to its own constituency, the shareholders.

With the help of management, the GM board annually reviews the skills and characteristics it desires, taking into account such issues as diversity, age, professional background, and international business experience.

The board should have a process to review its own performance. It needs to determine systematically whether it is adequately monitoring management and providing effective counsel. The GM board now does this annually, with an established process and specific criteria, including input from the CEO. It reviews the board's performance as a whole, not that of individual directors. The review includes consideration of areas in which the board or management believes a better contribution could be made.

The board's independent directors should conduct regularly scheduled reviews of the CEO's and key executives' performance. Reviews should be based on established, objective criteria, including the performance of the business, the accomplishment of long-term strategic business objectives, and the development of managers. GM's independent directors do reviews annually in executive session and report the results immediately to the CEO.

The board must understand and fully endorse the company's long-term strategies. This is not usurping management's job. The board must know the business well enough to be able to participate in forming the company's vision and direction. It must know enough to be able to arrive at an independent judgment of the soundness of the company's strategies for the future and to exercise the oversight necessary to fulfill its responsibilities to the owners.

The board must devote adequate time and attention to its single most important responsibility: selection of the CEO. The GM board, in addition, gets an annual report on succession planning from the CEO, which includes recommendations for successors to senior managers in the event that any are unexpectedly disabled. The CEO also gives a management-development report at the same time.

I realize that these views on corporate governance are by no means universally shared. Some chief executive officers are skeptical of the need for boards of directors to have their own policies or guidelines. They sense that somehow the process means a transfer of power from management to the board—and that, as a result, boards are going to get closer to running the business than, ideally, they should.

In theory, there is no transfer of power, even if some seems to be implied in this process. Boards have always had the same responsibilities. The only difference is in how they have executed them. In the past, boards have often depended on management "to do the right thing for the business." Some have passively deferred to a strong CEO's philosophy of "support me or kick me out." I don't think that's a very good way to operate. It may have worked for most companies most of the time. But whenever it didn't, the board usually found out too late. In most cases when businesses get into trouble, the problems do not show up overnight. They fester for some time. Owners of the business ought to expect their directors to be close enough to what's going on to recognize problems in time and to encourage change and correction—and not to let things get to the point where the only course is the "nuclear option" of replacing the management.

Directors need to develop independently a deep understanding of the company's strategies and plans for the future. Anything short of that simply won't enable them to recognize incipient problems and do something about them before they become acute. Reliance on the CEO's judgment alone is not sufficient to fulfill the directors' responsibilities.

Directors must have access to managers below the CEO. However, directors should confer with them only with the CEO's knowledge. GM's directors can call on managers at any time they choose, and the process is well accepted and practiced with discretion.

At GM, senior managers routinely attend the regular full-board meetings (not the executive sessions), and other managers are invited when relevant subjects are under consideration. Candid and perceptive dialogue, not just a review of oral and written reports, is useful for both the board and management.

Certainly, in advocating that directors should have more independence and should actively monitor management, I don't mean to suggest that they should have an adversarial relationship with management. Rather, it should be a sympathetic and productive relationship because the board has an important role in helping management succeed. Mutual respect and trust between the directors and the CEO are essential for a board to be productive.

Strong boards consisting of directors who take their obligations to owners seriously and work at their responsibilities should not be a threat to management. The truth is exactly the reverse. Strong boards can be a source of strength to management. As such, they also can be a source of competitive advantage to the company. The board is responsible for the successful perpetuation of the corporation. That responsibility cannot be relegated to management.

ALAN J. PATRICOF *is chairman and founder of Patricof & Co., the U.S. member of Apax Partners.*

As a venture capitalist, I have represented private equity investors on the boards of companies for many years. During my career, I have also served as an independent director on the boards of both public and private companies. These varying roles have highlighted for me how difficult it is to be independent if you don't adopt the attitudes and independence associated with ownership. I believe

In order to introduce truly independent attitudes to the boards of public companies, changes have to be made through laws, regulations, and/or voluntary guidelines.

that in order to introduce truly independent attitudes to the boards of public companies, changes have to be made through laws, regulations, and/or voluntary guidelines.

Whether actions to strengthen the hand of independent directors are taken by the stock exchanges, the Securities and Exchange Commission, the National Association of Securities Dealers, the Business Roundtable, or the Business Law Section of the Bar, they must be taken by someone. Long overdue are measures to ensure that ownership is faithfully represented in the corporate boardroom and to create safe harbors where independent directors can express views that differ from management's.

Even if outside directors dominate a given board in numbers, it's very tough to be a truly independent director. If outside directors really try to exercise their independence and do what they think is right, sooner or later they will clash with management. Although I strongly believe that outside directors should not create strategy or run the business, they must be able to influence management decisions.

The best CEO is a strong entrepreneurial leader who is firm in running the business and yet open-minded. He or she is someone who has a great deal of self-confidence, a great understanding of the particular business, and an ability to listen seriously to well-thought-out advice without feeling threatened. Such a CEO appreciates the fact that a director who is on the outside looking in can see what management cannot.

But many CEOs have trouble taking advice from any outsider, let alone from men and women whose involvement in the business is limited to attending four to six board meetings per year. They don't hold their boards in sufficiently high esteem. Deep down, they really wish they didn't have boards. That's why, at the end of the day, most independent directors get neutralized in one fashion or another.

Most outside directors face another obstacle in trying to maintain their independence. Their professional business relationship with the CEO becomes subsumed by a personal relationship. It's inevitable. When CEOs want something, they have a tendency to make it personal. For example, when a board's compensation committee is considering the CEO's salary or an executive-compensation program, many CEOs will lobby each committee member individually. Such one-on-one discussions put the independent director in a compromising position.

The more that the business aspect of the relationship is preserved and the social aspect is restricted, the greater is the likelihood that the outside director will be able to preserve his or her independence. But is this idealistic and not achievable in the real world? Guidelines similar to insider-trading rules, which specify how to behave under certain circumstances, would help. For example, they might stipulate that the CEO could discuss his or her salary only with the board's compensation committee as a whole. There could be similar rules for sensitive issues handled by the board's audit and nominating committees.

There also should be more extensive guidelines or regulations on what the composition of supposedly independent committees should be and what resources they should have available to them. The SEC might specify such ground rules.

The nominating committee is the one that ultimately has the greatest opportunity to influence the role of the board. Its authority over all aspects of board composition, compensation, procedures, and rules, including safeguards to ensure the board's independence, could be strengthened significantly at many companies. Indeed, boards might even consider the possibility of giving the committee explicit responsibility for overseeing all aspects of directors' independence. They might even want to rename it "the nominating and governance committee."

Outside directors, especially those serving on critical committees, should be required to have certain skills. Certainly, they should know how to read a financial statement and should be able to understand the finances and economics of the business. Perhaps an independent agency similar to that in Britain could be established to certify independent directors. Shareholders would have greater confidence in boards whose members were drawn from a pool of certified directors.

Many boards continue to have directors whose only qualification is that they are friends of the CEO. How can they truly serve as watch-dogs and provide the functions required for guidance and oversight?

For outside directors to be effective watchdogs, board committees also must be able without management's permission to call on outside specialists who can provide truly objective assessments of a company's internal operations. The compensation committee, for example, should be responsible for engaging compensation consultants to provide an unbiased view of senior management compensation in light of corporate performance, shareholder returns, and marketplace competitiveness. Compensation consultants engaged by management understandably feel pressured to be responsive primarily to management concerns like justifying pay increases. The recent SEC proxy disclosure rules, which have imposed certain requirements on compensation committees, have begun to ameliorate that situation. But perhaps if compensation consultants were hired by the independent directors on a three-year basis (rather than by management for a specific assignment), they would be more inclined to recommend holding the line on salary increases when appropriate and would feel freer to give objective advice.

Certain safe harbors also need to be established to allow outside directors to operate on a more independent basis. The kind of safe harbors I have in mind would make it easier for outside directors to speak up without having to worry as much as they do now about criticism and litigation. Litigation reform is being discussed broadly in the United States today and should help to remedy this problem.

Limits on both the minimum and the maximum time a director could serve would also encourage directors to act independently. After a certain period of time, a board, like any other organization that remains too constant, becomes inbred. The only way to change that is to have term limits. A minimum of three years and a maximum of ten would provide for continuity as well as turnover and would break down some of the clubbiness of boards. (Another idea, which admittedly is only a palliative but which sometimes can affect group dynamics dramatically, is to change where directors sit and whom they sit next to at board meetings.)

I believe that there is a regulation stipulating that if a board member declines to stand for reelection or resigns because of a disagreement with management, that person has the right to put comments in the proxy statement. This rule would be strengthened if a company were required to include in the proxy statement the departing director's voting record on issues that had been brought up in board meetings over the previous three years. It might even be a good idea to give all directors, whether leaving or remaining on the board, the right to register in the proxy statement their dissent on particular issues.

There also should be a voluntary guideline that encourages companies to establish formal programs aimed at making senior managers below the CEO feel comfortable in talking freely with outside directors. For example, it could be established as an automatic procedure that top officers meet separately with the outside directors once a year. Clearly the CEO would remain the major source of directors' knowledge about what is happening inside the company. But such a dialogue with other managers would certainly give directors greater insights into the company's operations. Some directors and executives might think that such a practice would undermine the CEO's relationship with his or her management team; but if it were required, there would be no negative connotations.

It is hard for outside directors not to be taken by surprise at some point, because they are dependent on the information that management prepares for them. To reduce the number of such surprises, many companies have installed what I consider to be a valuable check and balance: internal auditors who report directly to the board's audit committee. Their examination and their tests of the company's financial accounting systems are typically more extensive and detailed than those conducted by the company's own auditing firm. The purpose is to give the outside directors, as well as the company itself, detailed and constructive insight into the internal workings of the business. The process in and of itself makes all the participants more sensitive to accountability.

Let me now turn to another important area: shareholders' involvement with boards. We ought to make it easier for significant owners to be represented on the boards of public companies. One way would be to permit an institutional or individual shareholder (with a stake of

5% or more) who has held company shares for more than one year to nominate a director through the company's proxy mechanism.

We also ought to make it easier for larger shareholders and outside directors to exchange views. To this end, boards might consider holding a semiannual meeting for larger shareholders in addition to the annual meeting for all shareholders. I am sure that many people would not consider such a meeting appropriate and that some outside directors might see it as an inconvenience. However, making institutional investors more actively involved in selecting and interacting with directors would help ensure directors' independence from the management and encourage institutions to take a longer-term perspective.

To align the interests of owners and directors, I also favor reducing directors' cash compensation and increasing the amount they are paid in stock options. There is no substitute for directors who have a personal stake in the ultimate performance of a company's shares.

Although legal modifications of our corporate board system are essential, to be truly successful, all stakeholders must be willing to modify their relationships both to the company and to each other.

DENYS HENDERSON, *formerly chairman and CEO of Imperial Chemical Industries, serves as nonexecutive chairman of ICI and of Zeneca, the company that was created in 1993 when ICI spun off its pharmaceuticals, agrochemicals, and specialty chemicals businesses. He is stepping down from those posts this spring, when he becomes the nonexecutive chairman of the Rank Organization.*

Some in the United States believe that giving the jobs of board chairman and CEO to two separate people can help strengthen corporate governance. In Britain, too, this view is gaining credence following the recent publication of the Cadbury Code of Conduct on the subject. From my own experience, I believe that success depends not only on having well-qualified people in both jobs but also on establishing their personal chemistry.

Obviously, there are two kinds of nonexecutive chairmen: the insider who previously served as CEO and the outsider who has never belonged to the company's management. The advantage of an outsider is that he can be thoroughly objective and, lacking both detailed knowledge of the company or long-standing relationships with its managers, is less likely to try to interfere with the CEO's job of running the business.

On the other hand, because the chairman who has been CEO has a much better database, he can hit the ground running. In my own case, it was difficult at first to give up day-to-day control because I was still very energetic, and it was clear that further change in the organization was required. I found it a considerable challenge to move from the "energy mode" to the "wisdom mode."

The success of the nonexecutive-chairman arrangement is heavily dependent on the chairman's relationship with the CEO. If the chemistry isn't good, the relationship isn't going to work. And if the relationship does not work, the board and the company are in serious trouble. It's a critical reason why the CEO has to be involved in choosing a new nonexecutive chairman, especially if that person is coming from outside. Outside directors may want to oversee the search for candidates, but the CEO has to understand what's going on and certainly has to be able to express his views.

It's important that the chairman and the CEO agree from the beginning what each person's role will be. The last thing you want is a bloody fight over turf. The agreement should be put down in writing and eventually approved by the board. But the process of thoroughly understanding each other's viewpoint is more important than the final text.

Fundamentally, the nonexecutive chairman's job is to manage the board, overseeing how it carries out its major responsibilities. These include monitoring the company's financial performance, ensuring that there is adequate succession planning for senior management positions, and constantly monitoring corporate strategy and management structure. I emphasize the word *monitor*. The notion that nonexecutive directors who meet only once a month should determine the company's strategic direction is, quite frankly, unrealistic.

But nonexecutive directors led by the chairman have not only the right but also the obligation to make sure that management constantly tests its basic assumptions. Is the company in the right business? Is it covering the right territories? Is management looking far enough ahead? Is the company sufficiently competitive in its areas of expertise? Is its benchmarking of competitors sufficiently rigorous? And, most importantly, is there a changing environment that means management should reconsider whether its strategies are still relevant?

The nonexecutive chairman and the CEO together should continually emphasize to top management and the board the importance of increasing shareholder value. To this end, they should make sure that managers running the businesses are consulted regularly on corporate matters (such as improving earnings per share, return on capital employed, and cash flow) and are improving those businesses for which they are personally accountable.

The two also should share responsibility for tending to important corporate relationships, including those with the other board directors, major institutional investors, the media, governments, employees, pensioners, and customers. The job of managing those relations as well as running the business has become so demanding

In my view, it is vital for the chairman and the CEO to have a close working relationship, which is why the chemistry between them is so important.

that it's now too much for one person. Having two people to handle them is one of the main advantages of splitting the top corporate responsibilities.

How much time does it take for a nonexecutive chairman to perform his job? If it's a big company with a wide variety of businesses, it probably will require between 75 and 100 days a year. If the chairman spends much more time than that, he's going to get into the CEO's hair. If he spends much less, he's not going to have the information he needs to be effective.

In my view, it is vital for the chairman and the CEO to have a close working relationship, which is why the chemistry between them is so important. The chairman and other outside directors should always be wary of doing anything that might undermine that relationship or damage the board's team approach to carrying out its responsibilities. For that reason, I feel strongly that they should not bypass the CEO to obtain information without his or her knowledge. If they believe they're not getting some critical information or that they are being misled, they should tell the CEO that they are dissatisfied and are going to get it themselves. At the end of the day, though, nonexecutive directors have to recognize that management is running the company. And if they feel dissatisfied, their ultimate sanction is to change the management.

BERNARD MARCUS *is chairman of The Home Depot.*

I'm a firm believer in having activist outside directors on the board. We, the top management of the Home Depot, tell our outside directors the good, the bad, and the ugly. For example, we recently had a five-hour board meeting during which we went through every phase of our operations. We shared our triumphs and our concerns for the present and future. But we don't expect our outside directors just to take our word for everything. We ask them to visit our stores by themselves and talk with associates and customers.

They each visit eight stores every quarter. The visits typically last one to two hours, but some directors stay even longer. About half announce over the public-address system that they are in the store and invite our associates or customers to talk to them. And some just walk around and have conversations. They find out how customers feel about our business and how our employees feel about the company and their working environment—what they're happy with and what they're unhappy with. For example, one director recently went to a group of stores and was told by the associates that the stores were understaffed. We'll investigate the matter. We pay close attention because we

We believe that a director who is intimately familiar with what's going on in our stores will have a better knowledge of our company.

believe it's important. It says to employees and customers that we listen and care about what's going on,
that what they think or feel is of concern to us. Outside
directors serve as another set of eyes. They help management find those things it's doing wrong.

Equally important, we believe that a director who is
intimately familiar with what's going on in our stores
will have a better understanding of our company. Our
outside directors—6 of our 10-member board are outside
directors—have a feel for the company that I suspect the
outside directors of many other companies are lacking.
How can outside directors constructively review management's strategy if they don't have a deep knowledge
of the business? How can they know whether what management is telling them about the business is true?
Unfortunately, the outside directors of many companies
are given just one side of the story.

And too many companies still pick directors for social
reasons. We don't. Every member of our board has a value
that is crucial to our current businesses or necessary for
our future. For example, one of the main reasons we
brought Don Keough of Coca-Cola onto our board was
our ambition to expand into other parts of the world. Don
has tremendous knowledge about other places and has
contacts all over the world. In addition, he's a marketing
genius, and we're in a marketing business.

I know that we ask our outside directors to commit a
lot more time than many companies ask theirs. But I
think an outside director who isn't willing to make a big
commitment is foolish to sit on a board, given the danger
of lawsuits that directors face these days. I, for one,
wouldn't do it.

To ensure that outside directors are willing to make a
genuine commitment, companies should require them to

make a meaningful investment in the company. Many companies listed on the New York Stock Exchange have board members with only 50 shares of the company. It's difficult for me to believe that such people can adequately represent shareholders.

When I go on the board of another company, I buy a minimum of 2,000 shares. And when people join our board, we insist that they make a personal and serious financial investment in the Home Depot—either by purchasing stock or by investing in an options program that we make available to them. It is important that the amount is significant enough that each person feels that he or she is at risk. Outside directors should feel that they have plenty to gain financially if the company succeeds and an equal amount to lose if it doesn't.

DAVID W. JOHNSON *is chairman, president, and chief executive officer of Campbell Soup Company. He has served as CEO of Entenmann's and of Gerber Products.*

Heightened accountability of managers—and directors—to owners is inevitable. Powerful forces are at work that ensure change, including global free trade, legally mandated comparisons of company performance with that of peers, and sophisticated and empowered share-holders. These forces will not be turned back. But managers and directors should not view this heightned accountability as a threat. It can unite owners, directors, and managers in a common drive for business excellence—for results that ensure prosperity for the enterprise.

Simply put, good corporate governance captures the unambiguous accountability of the best-run LBOs and private companies and applies it to large public companies. Knowing that anxieties can be stilled only in the specific, I offer a possible model to guide us. It is expressed in a series of negotiable propositions that a new CEO, seeking to establish a constructive relationship, might write to the board of directors. The letter might read as follows.

Dear Members of the Board: I want to work with you in a partnership that will feature both your independence to represent the interests of shareholders and my capability to lead the organization and measurably drive long-term results. In this context, I would suggest that your key responsibilities are these:

- *To evaluate and advise on my recommendations for strategic directions and plans.*

- *To evaluate annually my work and succession plans, as well as the capabilities of the organization to move in the agreed strategic direction. These evaluations should be formal, beginning with the compensation committee but requiring review by the full board. In this context, I endorse the idea of having a lead director who would chair meetings as appropriate—for example, when the CEO's performance is being evaluated.*

- *To construct a motivational framework of rewards that will focus on results that build long-term shareholder wealth.*

My key responsibilities would be:

- *To develop strategies that would deliver strong market franchises as well as superior long-term financial results. In this context, organizational and development plans should serve as coordinates for strategy and accomplishment.*

- *To measure the best competitive practices and inform you of comparative trends.*

- *To inform you regularly of the status of the key initiatives necessary to deliver the annual plan and of longer-term milestones to check the strategic course of the enterprise.*

Together we should operate in an atmosphere of constructive discontent—tapping the positive tension that comes from shared values but distinct accountabilities. Our joint aim should be to achieve competitive excellence and thus deliver superior rewards to shareholders.

Our board should include no more than two members of management—the CEO and the CEO's probable successor. Committees such as audit, compensation, and nominating (or governance) should consist entirely of independent directors. The CEO should be actively involved as a pivot and resource for such committees.

We need written criteria for selecting directors. The core criterion should always be a proven track record of performance—whether in business management, R&D, nonprofits, or the academic world. The proof of excellence is in leadership and the results it offers the organization. To unify board members' aspirations for our company, the major component of compensation should be in stock or stock options. Board members also should be required to buy and keep a substantial stake in our company's stock, just as senior executives are required to do.

Committee assignments should be calculated in part to build the skills of directors and the board as a whole. Each committee needs to include members who have special skills relevant to its work. Equally valuable for the long term are members with other experiences who are assigned to the committee to learn and to cross-fertilize.

Together we should ensure sharing of information and ideas between directors and the executive, going beyond the review of annual and strategic plans to embrace innovation, new products, possible acquisitions, and other strategic or significant company initiatives. Such sharing should enhance the partnership I seek.

Sincerely,
The CEO

Good corporate governance is a powerful force to build business excellence. It elevates board competence and guides teamwork. The greatest gain is for shareholders.

Originally published in March–April 1995
Reprint 95208

About the Contributors

JAY A. CONGER is Professor of Organizational Behavior at London Business School and a Senior Research Scientist at the Center for Effective Organizations at the University of Southern California. He has also taught on the faculties of Harvard, INSEAD, and McGill Universities. His research interests include executive leadership, the management of organizational change, charismatic leadership, boardroom dynamics, and the training and development of leadership ability. He has published extensively in journals such as *The Academy of Management Review*, *Harvard Business Review*, *Journal of Organizational Behavior*, and *Human Resources Management Review*, and is the author of eight books including *Winning 'Em Over*, *Learning to Lead*, and his most recent, *Building Leaders*.

GORDON DONALDSON is the Willard Prescott Smith Professor of Corporate Finance, Emeritus, and former Senior Associate Dean at the Harvard Business School. Prior to joining the Harvard Business School in 1955, he served on the faculty of the School of Commerce at the University of Manitoba, Canada. His most recent teaching assignment was in the Owner-President Management Program. He has also taught in other Executive programs, in the MBA program, and in the Doctoral program. Professor Donaldson is the author of several books including, most recently, *Corporate Restructuring*,

Managing Corporate Wealth, and *Decision Making at the Top* (with Jay Lorsch).

DAVID FINEGOLD is Assistant Research Professor at the University of Southern California Marshall School of Business in the Center for Effective Organization. He is an expert on the relationship between the skills of the workforce and economic performance in advanced industrial countries. His work has focused on the impact of globalization and technological change on skill demands and the changing employment relationship. His two most recent books are *Are Skills the Answer? The Political Economy of Skill-Creation in the Advanced Industrial Countries* and *The German Skills Machine in Comparative Perspective.*

RAKESH KHURANA is an Assistant Professor of Management at MIT's Sloan School of Management. His primary research focuses on the dynamics of the CEO labor market and issues related to corporate governance. His more recent work explores the link between intermediary market institutions, such as executive search firms, and CEO tenure and CEO pay.

EDWARD E. LAWLER III is a Professor and Director of the Center for Effective Organizations at the University of Southern California Marshall School of Business. Prior to his time at University of Southern California, he served on the faculties of Yale and University of Michigan. He has been honored by many professional organizations in his field and is the author or coauthor of over 200 articles and 30 books, including *From the Ground Up* and *Rewarding Excellence.*

JAY W. LORSCH is the Louis Kirstein Professor of Human Relations, Chairman of Doctoral Programs, and Director of Research at Harvard Business School. He is the author or coauthor of over a dozen books including his most recent publication, *Pawns or Potentates*, which focuses on corporate boards, and *Organizations and Environment*, with Paul R. Lawrence, which won the Academy of Management's Best Management Book of the Year Award and the James A. Hamilton Book Award of the College of Hospital Administrators. He has taught in all of Harvard Business School's executive education programs, and has served as Senior Associate Dean, Chairman of the Advanced Management Programs, Chairman of the Organizational Behavior Area, and Chairman of Doctoral Programs.

WALTER J. SALMON is the Stanley Roth Sr. Professor of Retailing, Emeritus, at Harvard Business School. He has been a member of the Harvard Business School faculty since 1956 and has served as Associate Dean for Faculty Affairs, Senior Associate Dean, and Director of External Relations. He is on the board of several major corporations including The Neiman Marcus Group, Hannaford Brothers Company, and Circuit City Stores. He is also a director of the Tufts Health Plan. His current research concerns trends in distribution, issues of organization, logistics, and information systems in retailing, and balancing consumer interests in breadth of selection with their interest in low prices.

At the time of the article's original publication, **JOHN POUND** was a visiting professor at the Harvard Law School and a chair of New Foundations, a multidisciplinary Harvard-based research project on corporate governance.

Note: *The information provided within each article about the contributors to perspectives and roundtables was applicable at the time of original publication.*

Index